Carlos Chávez

MEXICO'S MODERN-DAY ORPHEUS

Twayne's Music Series

Chris Frigon and Camille Roman,
Consulting Editors

Carlos Chávez

MEXICO'S MODERN-DAY ORPHEUS

Robert L. Parker

Twayne Publishers

Carlos Chávez
MEXICO'S MODERN-DAY ORPHEUS

Robert L. Parker

Copyright © 1983
by G.K. Hall & Company
All Rights Reserved

Published in 1983
by Twayne Publishers
A Division of G. K. Hall & Company
70 Lincoln Street, Boston, Massachusetts 02111

Printed on permanent/durable
acid-free paper and bound in
the United States of America.

First Printing

This book was designed by
Barbara Anderson and typeset
in Bauer Bodoni by Compset, Inc.,
with Onyx display type supplied
by Solotype Typographers.

0-8057-9455-7

Contents

Carlos Chávez photographed at his home in Las Lomas de Chapultepec, 1962.
Collection of Donald Hunstein

About the Author

The author is currently assistant dean of the School of Music and professor of music at the University of Miami, Coral Gables, Florida. A native of New Mexico, he attended elementary and secondary schools in Albuquerque and Raton, and in El Paso, Texas. He received a bachelor's degree from Baylor University with majors in history and music theory and a minor in Spanish, and Master of Music and Ph.D. degrees from The University of Texas. He has been a professional trumpet player and arranger since 1947, has performed with the El Paso, Corpus Christi, and Houston Symphony Orchestras, the United States Fourth Army Band, in numerous musical theater, show, and jazz orchestras, and was founding director of the Houston Jazz Ensemble, an affiliate of Young Audiences Incorporated. He is a member of the American Federation of Musicians, the American Musicological Society, and the Society for Music Theory.

He is editor of *The Collected Works of Adam Rener* (two volumes to date) and a modern critical edition of Reformation choral music, *Officia Paschalia, Wittenberg, 1539* (Kassel: Bärenreiter Verlag, in press). Research for these editions has been supported by grants from the German Academic Exchange Service and the Ludwig Vogelstein Foundation. The recent *Academic American Encyclopedia* contains fourteen biographical articles by the author on composers from the fifteenth century to modern times.

The author has been a longtime devotee of Carlos Chávez's music. He prepared an analytical study of the composer's first three symphonies as a master's thesis in music theory in 1956. The present study marks a concentrated return by the author—a kind of "Chávez revisited"—to a subject of major interest to him and one that figures as an important part of the large picture in contemporary music.

Preface

The Revolution of 1910 shook cultural life in Mexico to its foundations. When the dust settled, about 1920, a new nationalistic movement in the arts began to take shape, and soon swept away the stultified, European-based style cultivated during Porfirio Díaz's dictatorship. The provocative murals of Rivera, Orozco, and Siqueiros decorating public buildings in Mexico City are evidence of how the revolution affected painting—riotous color, bold strokes, neoprimitivism, and violent political statements against the yoke of tyranny imposed on Mexico since the Spanish conquest.

Carlos Chávez (1899–1978) was the first Mexican composer to enunciate this new nationalism. With great talent, energy, and flourish, he was able to make himself highly visible in Mexico City and then in New York City in the 1920s. He was soon recognized as a progressive voice in American music by composers like Aaron Copland, Edgard Varèse, and Henry Cowell in New York, and Manuel Ponce in Mexico. He organized the first permanent symphony orchestra in Mexico and directed it for twenty-one seasons. As director of the National Conservatory and chief of the Department of Fine Arts in the Secretariat of Public Education he was able to renovate Mexico's outmoded instruction in the arts and to infuse it with rich resources from pre-Conquest culture.

Chávez's international reputation was launched in 1936 when he conducted the CBS Radio Orchestra in the world premiere of his *Sinfonía India* in New York. The popularity of this fresh and exotic work, and his demonstrated ability at orchestral direction, opened doors for performances of his music and invitations to conduct the major orchestras of the Americas and Europe. In a career spanning over fifty years, he composed more than 200 works, conducted in excess of 100 orchestras, presented well over 100 public lectures, and authored numerous essays on music, aesthetics, and pedagogy. Like Orpheus, the legendary musician whose playing of the lyre made trees dance and rivers stand still, Chávez made extraordinary things happen with his music and music making in Mexico.

The present study is a survey of that active musical and administrative career and its productivity. Events concerning his life and work are addressed chronologically in Chapter 1. Chapters 2 through 7 are each devoted to a classification of works from which representative examples are individually examined. In the selection of the approximately fifty compositions discussed, an attempt was made to include all of the works that had been recorded commercially by the time of this writing. With few exceptions, those included are also published. The few that have been neither recorded nor published were selected because of their historical or musical significance, an unavoidably subjective choice. The unpublished compositions included were examined in the Performing Arts Library at Lincoln Center for the Performing Arts (where most of the manuscripts are now permanently located), in the Library of Congress, and in the case of the *Trombone Concerto*, by means of Per Brevig's fair copy of the score. Chapter 8 contains a summary of Chávez's activities—composing, conducting, administration, writing, his personality, and an assessment of his place in music, both in Mexico and worldwide, given the limited historical perspective at hand. Also included in this survey are an abbreviated chronology, a listing of the orchestras Chávez conducted, and, as backmatter, a catalog of works and discography.

Much has been written by Chávez and about him. The most complete in the latter category is Roberto García Morillo's life and works biography which was prepared in close cooperation with the Mexican composer and with material supplied by him. Although Chávez obviously exercised some control of its content, García Morillo's book remains the most comprehensive for information up to the time of its completion in 1960. Rodolfo Halffter's complete catalog of (Chávez's) works, commissioned and published by the Society of Authors and Composers of Music in Mexico, is a thorough, detailed piece of scholarship, but it does not cover works written after 1969. The composer's daughter, Anita Chávez, has provided a curriculum vitae which has been useful in filling in the periods not covered by García Morillo's and Halffter's work. The National Institute of Fine Arts in Mexico published the papers and testimonials presented at the first national homage to the composer shortly after his death. This volume gives current attitudes about Chávez held by prominent musicians from Mexico and the United States. Unavailable at the time of this writing were the composer's personal papers and correspondence. These documents, preserved in the Mexican National Archive, will be a valuable aid to further investigation in the future.

Surveys of Mexican, Latin American, and American music by Chase, Copland, Thomson, Slonimsky, Stevenson, Béhague, and Malmström have helped to establish Chávez's position and direction in relation to composers of the same era and geographical setting, and to evaluate his work in an historical context. In dealing with a subject as recent as Carlos Chávez, it would be amiss not to seek comments and opinions from his family and associates. To that end, the material presented herein incorporates information received in the form of interviews and conversations, and letters to this writer. This direct communication lends currency and is of help in capturing the human side of the subject; among its potential risks are personal bias and inaccurate memory on the part of those communicating or reporting.

Of the many people who have been helpful with this undertaking, the author first wishes to thank Anita Chávez for her enthusiastic support and for her generosity in providing data and materials. Miguel Coelho and Julián Orbón have given expert advice and material which has illuminated a number of dark corners. To those who responded by mail or agreed to interviews, a special word of thanks is in order. Among these, in addition to those already mentioned, are Herbert Barrett, Paul Bowles, Frank Campbell, Antonio Castro Leal, Manuel de la Cera Alonso, Arthur Cohn, Paul Christensen, Aaron Copland, David Diamond, Manuel Enríquez S., Robert Floyd, Carolina Amor Fornier, Ellis Freedman, Blas Galindo, Gilbert Johnson, Normand Lockwood, William Lichtenwanger, Archibald MacLeish, Luciano Magnanini, Alan Marks, Carlos Luis Martínez, William Masselos, Eduardo and Mari Carmen Mata, Humberto Hernández Medrano, Olga Morales, Vivien Perlis, Hector Quintanar, María Teresa Rodríguez, William Schuman, José Serebrier, Nicholas Slonimsky, Henryk Szeryng, Virgil Thomson, and Laura Villaseñor.

The author is indebted to Susan Potter for her careful reading of the manuscript and thoughtful suggestions, to Renée Gordon for her untiring effort in preparing the typescript, and for assistance in this task to Cheryl Sánchez. The University of Miami is also to be thanked for a sabbatical leave which allowed released time to collect data in Mexico City, Washington, D.C., and New York. Finally, *muchísimas gracias* to the editors of the Twayne Musical Arts Series— Caroline Birdsall, and John LaBine—for unfailing patience and guidance in seeing this work to completion.

Life in Mexico was a vital force in shaping the musical personality of Carlos Chávez. Its unique history, political interworkings, and cultural climate had many obvious effects on his career, but the more subtle effects may sometimes elude the eye of the "north-of-border" observer. The author's main purpose will be served if he manages to introduce the music of this unique Mexican artist to some who were unfamiliar with it, or if a bit of new information and enjoyment comes through to those already acquainted with his work.

Robert L. Parker

University of Miami

Chronology

1899 Carlos Chávez is born in Popotla, a northwest suburb of Mexico City, June 13.

1909 Studies piano with composer Manuel M. Ponce, until 1913.

1915 Studies piano with Pedro Luis Ogazón, until 1920.

1917 Studies harmony with Juan B. Fuentes, until 1918.

1920 Receives first publication of his music (for piano).

1921 First public performance of his music (in Mexico City). First major commission: the ballet *El Fuego Nuevo* [The New Fire].

1922 Marries Otilia Ortiz, September 1. Travels with wife to Vienna, Berlin, and Paris, September, 1922, to April, 1923.

1923 Daughter Anita is born, June 5. First sojourn to New York City, December, 1923, until March, 1924.

1925 Son Augustín is born, February 11. Directs Concerts of New Music in Mexico City, December, 1925, until early 1926.

1926 Second sojourn to New York City, September, 1926, until July, 1928.

1928 Becomes musical director of the Symphony Orchestra of Mexico; remains twenty-one seasons. Assumes directorship of the Mexican National Conservatory of Music, December, 1928, until March, 1933, (and again May, 1934, until December, 1934).

1929 Daughter Juanita is born, December 18.

1933 Becomes chief of the Department of Fine Arts in the Secretariat of Public Education in Mexico, March, 1933, to May, 1934.

1936 Begins guest conducting major U.S. and Latin American orchestras. Premieres his *Sinfonía India* [Indian Symphony] with the CBS Radio Orchestra in New York, January 23.

1937 W. W. Norton publishes his book *Toward a New Music*.

1938 Receives his first of two John Simon Guggenheim Foundation Grants for composition.

1940 Commissioned by Nelson Rockefeller to organize concerts of Mexican music in the New York Museum of Modern Art, beginning March 16.

1943 Elected a charter member of the National College of Mexico along with distinguished artists Diego Rivera and José Orozco.

1944 Mutual Radio Network broadcasts the Symphony Orchestra of Mexico in a summer series each Sunday night.

1947 Becomes director of the National Institute of Fine Arts, January.

1948 Serves his final season as director of the Symphony Orchestra of Mexico.

1949 Organizes the National Symphony Orchestra of Mexico within the Institute of Fine Arts; names Moncayo as director. First return to Europe since 1923; accepts UNESCO commission to write two piano works.

1952 Relinquishes directorship of the National Institute of Fine Arts to concentrate on composing and conducting.

1953 Teaches at Berkshire Music Festival, Tanglewood, Mass.

1956 Receives his second Guggenheim Foundation Grant.

1958 Becomes "Slee" Visiting Professor of Music at the University of Buffalo, N.Y., February to May. Occupies the Charles Eliot Norton Poetic Chair at Harvard University, October, 1958, to April, 1959; lectures published by Harvard University Press as *Musical Thought*.

1959 Commissioned by the New York Philharmonic to write an orchestral work for the opening of Lincoln Center *(Symphony No. 6)*.

1960 Founds and directs the Chávez Composition Workshop in the National Conservatory of Mexico, until 1964.

1962 Guest conducts thirteen orchestras in Europe, Latin America, and the United States.

1964 Receives a commission to write an orchestral piece for the opening of the National Museum of Anthropology in Mexico City: *Resonancias* [Resonances].

1965   Commission from the Southwest Radio Network of West Germany for an orchestral piece *(Soli III)*.

1966   Accepts invitation to teach composition at the University of California, March through May.

1967   Composes *Elatio* [Elation] for orchestra to commemorate the restoration of the Mexican Republic (1867).

1968   Receives the International Koussevitsky Prize for the (Columbia) recording of his six symphonies.

1969   Daughter Juanita dies after complications following surgery in Mexico City.

1970   Directs the Cabrillo Music Festival in Aptos, California, for first of four consecutive seasons.

1971   Named advisor to the President of Mexico, Luis Echeverría.

1972   Accepts invitation to conduct his *Sinfonía India* for video taping in Munich to promote Olympiad XX.

1973   Appointed director of the Department of Music of the National Institute of Fine Arts and director of the National Symphony Orchestra of Mexico, both in January; resigns both posts the same month.

1974   Seventy-fifth birthday celebration concert in Chopin Hall, Mexico City.

1975   Elected honorary president of the International Conference of Music and Communication, held in Mexico City, September 3 to 10.

1977   Named advisor to Mexican President José López Portillo, May 19.

1978   Wife dies, April 28, 1978. Final conducting appearance: Interamerican Music Festival, Kennedy Center, Washington, D.C., May 9. Receives honorary Doctor of Arts degree from Columbia College, Chicago, Illinois, June 2. Succumbs to lengthy illness, August 2. Homage presented in the Rotunda of Illustrious Men, Mexico City, August 3. Official national homage begins with a concert at the Palace of Fine Arts, August 27.

1

Biography

Carlos Chávez was one of the first artists to articulate the post-Revolutionary spirit in Mexico in the early 1920s. He founded the country's first permanent symphony orchestra and directed both the National Conservatory of Music and the National Institute of Fine Arts. He invented a nationalistic musical style that has had worldwide appeal and he transformed Mexican musical elements into a universal and uniquely personal idiom. Chávez is recognized as the leading musician of Mexico in this century and as one of the three major composers in all of Latin America, along with Heitor Villa-Lobos and Alberto Ginastera. In a conducting career that spanned over fifty years, he directed most of the major orchestras in the United States, Latin America, and Europe and was acclaimed for his broad knowledge of orchestral literature and his fidelity of interpretation.

Early Life

Carlos Chávez (his full name was Carlos Antonio de Padua Chávez y Ramírez) was born June 13, 1899, in Popotla, a northwest suburb of Mexico City. His father Augustín, an inventor, died about 1904, leaving the mother Juvencia to care for Carlos and five older children.[1] Most if not all of the ancestors were *criollos* ("creoles"), that is, descended from early Spanish settlers in Mexico. But Chávez biographer Roberto García Morillo believes there may have been some Indian blood on the maternal side.[2]

The family lived at Casa No. 2, de la Calle Real in Popotla near the Normal School for Young Women which Juvencia Chávez directed. As the Revolution of 1910 intensified, school teachers were ordered, in 1915, to leave Mexico City. The Chávez family relocated in Veracruz from February to August, 1915. By then Juvencia and all six children were on the federal payroll as teachers under the Secretariat of Public Education. Carlos, who was sixteen at the time, would

1

commute to Mexico City periodically to pick up the family paychecks. On one such trip he narrowly missed being struck by a stray bullet from a skirmish between the opposing forces of Venustiano Carranza and Emiliano Zapata.[3] Despite the upheaval and peril of the Revolution, the family survived and resumed life in the capital city.

Musical Education

Carlos Chávez began piano study with his brother Manuel at about nine or ten years of age, and he continued briefly after that with Asunción Para. From 1910 to 1913 he was a piano pupil of composer Manuel M. Ponce. But Pedro Luís Ogazón, a disciple of Joseph Hofmann, is the teacher Chávez credits with introducing him to the best classical and romantic music, and with developing his musical taste and technical formation. Chávez met him shortly after returning to Mexico City in 1915. Ogazón, who gave weekly recitals in his home in the San Angel district of Mexico City, was the first person to introduce Debussy's music in Mexico (in 1903).

It was through Ogazón that Chávez met his harmony teacher Juan B. Fuentes. Fuentes had written a book on harmony which Chávez admired for its simplicity in explaining ideas and concepts which he felt earlier and more celebrated writers had overcomplicated or had made too rigid in their application. The earlier writers included Jahdasson, Richter, Durand, and Riemann, all considered to be authorities at the time.

Venting the Creative Urge

Chávez started composing on his own when he began his piano studies. A few years later, he began to improvise at the piano, playing fanciful musings for his own enjoyment.[4]

Chávez did not see any value in seeking out a composition teacher. He preferred to study by analyzing works of the great masters (García Morillo, 13). He summed up the composition instruction available in Mexico during his youth in a 1977 interview by saying "there were only two teachers of composition [Gustavo] Campa and [Rafael] Tello. Both were teaching composition at the National Conservatory . . . their music was a weak reflection of French, Italian nineteenth-century music." He went on to say that their methods of teaching were not convincing to him, even as young as he was: two years of solfege followed by two years of harmony, followed by two years of counterpoint and fugue and one year of musical form. After these seven years, the student received two more years of composition study before earning a diploma in composition.

At age twelve, Carlos and his friend Raul Lozano scoured Albert Guiraud's *Traité d'Instrumentation et Orchestration* "page by page," and the two of them were able to read orchestral scores of Beethoven, Wagner, and Debussy at the piano. At fifteen he began composing his first symphony, making and revising sketches, writing and rewriting pages. After two years, he had completed two (of its eventual three) movements. Up to this point, he had heard a symphony orchestra only once, in the 1909–1910 season of the National Conservatory Orchestra conducted by Carlos Meneses. He completed the symphony in 1918.[5]

The indigenous Indian music Chávez heard on frequent family excursions to nearby Tlaxcala had significant bearing on his later compositional direction. As the Mexican revolution surged after 1910, Chávez became heir to the renascence which began to prevade the arts. Caught up in the spirit of this artistic movement, he wrote, at age sixteen, an article entitled "The Present Importance of the Flowering of National Music" published in the periodical *Gladios*[6] in 1916, in which he defended his feeling of restlessness for music with a Mexican orientation (García Morillo, 14).

Most of Chávez's compositions before 1921 were derivative of European Classical and Romantic models as their titles reflect: *Prelude and Fugue* and *Sonata Fantasia* (1917); *Gavota* (1918). But his early output also includes arrangements of revolutionary and traditional Mexican songs, showing an important step toward the solid nationalistic stance he would reach in the mid-1920s. Among these nationalistic pieces are *Adelita y La Cucaracha* (1915), *Adiós, Adiós* (1919), and *Las Margaritas* (1919). An early milestone was reached in 1920 when the firm of Wagner and Levien in Mexico City published a half-dozen of his pieces mostly for solo piano. The composer was coming of age.

Coming of Age—The 1920s

In 1921, Carlos Chávez presented the first public concert of his music. The program included his *Sextet for Strings and Piano*, some songs and some solo piano music. In a review of the concert, Manuel Ponce remarked that his former pupil had come under the "double influence of romanticism of the Schumann, Chopin type, and modernism which attracts with its aura of novelty and exoticism" (García Morillo, 17). Certainly, Chávez's music stood out sharply against the prevailing conservatism still holding over from the regime of Porfirio Díaz. Composers like Tello and Meneses, who perpetuated nineteenth-century traditions, were in control of musical life in Mexico in 1921. Chávez saw that, if he were to succeed, it would have to be without the help of the reigning musical establishment. Fortunately, the revolution at that time began to bear fruit culturally in ways which aided Chávez's cause.

Incipient Nationalism

When Álvaro Obregón became President of Mexico in 1921, he allocated a large budget for the Secretariat of Public Education. As secretary for this important branch of government he reinstated José Vasconcelos, one of the leading intellectuals in Mexico. In keeping with his support of the artistic renascence growing out of the revolution, Vasconcelos began to underwrite the rebirth of painting in Mexico by commissioning the decoration of refurbished buildings like the church and convent of San Pedro and the National Preparatory School with murals by Diego Rivera, José Clemente Orozco, and David Alfaro Siqueiros.[7] In 1921, Vasconcelos asked Chávez to compose a ballet based on themes of ancient Aztec culture.[8]

Chávez found, after some searching, a legend in Aztec mythology which he considered appropriate for the commission. Specifically, his ballet, entitled *El Fuego Nuevo* [The New Fire], was drawn from a ceremony signifying the renewal of life, after a fifty-two-year Aztec century, by means of a new gift of fire from the gods. Through his recollections of the indigenous music of Tlaxcala, the composer was able to evoke a hitherto unknown symphonic sonority of strikingly neoprimitive character without quoting a single Indian theme. His attempt to get an instrumental reading of the work by Julian Carillo's Orquesta Sinfónica was unsuccessful despite Vasconcelos's recommendation.[9] In fact, the music was not performed until 1928 when Chávez led the Orquesta Sinfónica de México (Symphony Orchestra of Mexico) in its premiere.

European Exploration

On September 1, 1922, the young Mexican composer married Otilia Ortiz. He had met Otilia through Luis Ogazón. She was one of Ogazón's most successful pupils and was already giving recitals in Mexico City. The couple set out immediately on a trip which took them to Vienna, Berlin, and Paris. The trip was for the twofold purpose of exploring musical conditions in Europe and, unquestionably, as a means of furthering Chávez's own career. Pianist Ignaz Friedman, who had become acquainted with Chávez's music in Mexico, recommended the publication of some of the music to Hertzka at Universal Editions in Vienna. However, Hertzka explained that due to the backlog of work at Universal, it would not be possible to print any of his music for two or three more years (García Morillo, 26). He was more fortunate with the firm of Bote und Bock in Berlin, which published his *Second Piano Sonata* and his piano arrangement of the traditional Mexican song "Las Mañanitas." In these two publications his name retains the final maternal appellation: Carlos Chávez y Ramírez.

Carlos and Otilia stayed in Vienna two weeks, in Berlin five months, and in Paris eight or ten days. In Paris he was unsuccessful in seeing his idol Maurice

Ravel; however, he did manage an audience with Paul Dukas who advised him to concentrate on the rich popular music of Mexico as Manuel de Falla had done with Spanish music.[10] He came away convinced that what he needed was not to be found in the academic and routine life in Europe, but more likely within the new ferment in the arts that had begun to manifest itself in Mexico. But he found the stranglehold of musical life in Mexico by the arch-conservatives a discouraging obstacle. After only a brief return to his native country, during which time his first child Anita was born (June 5, 1923), he set out alone in December for New York City. The family remained behind at the home of Otilia's mother.

Otilia assumed a role conducive to the development of her husband's artistic capacities. She gave up her own career as a concert pianist, took care of the family, and resigned herself to the absences of her husband necessitated by his profession. She protected the privacy required for his work; the children "practically had to make an appointment to see their father." A multilinguist, Otilia spoke Spanish, English, French, German (her mother was a native German), and Italian. She was to remain a constant source of strength to her husband and family.[11]

The Journeyman Years

During his four month stay in New York (which lasted until March, 1924), Chávez was impressed by the quality of the orchestras, the advanced state of electronics relating to music, and the spontaneity of jazz music. He returned to Mexico City after this brief exploration, but the positive reaction to what he observed in New York helped precipitate his return there in 1926.

Back in Mexico City, Chávez moved his family to his mother's home at San Luis Potosí 188. He organized Concerts of New Music in 1924 at the National Preparatory School and reinstituted them the next season, from December, 1925, through the first few months of 1926. These concerts consisting of mostly chamber music, followed along the same lines as those being presented regularly in New York by the International Composers' Guild and the League of Composers. With management assistance from Ricardo Ortega and musical collaboration with singer Lupe Medina de Ortega and violinist Silvestre Revueltas, Chávez introduced modern music which had never before been heard in Mexico. Composers whose works were performed include Auric, Bartók, Debussy, Falla, Honegger, Milhaud, Poulenc, Revueltas, Satie, Schoenberg, Stravinsky, Varèse, in addition to Chávez himself: *String Quartet No. 1* (1921) (García Morillo, 39). The moderate success of these concerts was not enough to dissuade Chávez from the feeling that musical progress in Mexico was too slow for him to remain. This attitude, reinforced with his earlier impressions of New York City, provided sufficient impetus for a return trip in September, 1926. Again his family, enlarged with the birth of son Augustán February 11, 1925, remained behind in Mexico for financial reasons.[12] He travelled to New York with Mexican painter Rufino Tamayo, and the two artists shared living quarters in Greenwich Village.

In New York, the composer attached himself to the progressive composition movement. Among those of this group who became close and lasting friends of Chávez were Aaron Copland and Edgard Varèse (the latter having commissioned his *Energía* for nine instruments in 1925).

Since returning from Europe in 1923, Chávez had amassed an ample portfolio of compositions. These works included: *Tres Exágonos* [Three Hexagons] for voice and piano, and a version for voice and small instrumental ensemble (1923); *Seven Pieces for Piano* (1923–1930); *Otros Tres Exágonos* [Another Three Hexagons] for voice and small ensemble (1924); *Sonatinas*, for piano, violin and piano, and cello and piano (1924); and the above mentioned *Energía* for nine instruments (1925). The "hard charm" and "indo-American doggedness" that Copland heard in these works[13] emerges without dependence on Mexican melodies. New York critic Paul Rosenfeld commented on Brahmsian and Schumannesque traits in the *Sonatina* for violin and Satie-like drollness in *36* from the *Seven Pieces for Piano*.[14]

Mature Nationalism

Chávez returned to Mexican subject matter for his ballets *Los Cuatro Soles* [The Four Epochs, 1925] and *Caballos de Vapor* [Horsepower, 1926]. The first of these, for large orchestra and Indian percussion instruments, depicts the four epochs of the Aztec calendar—water, wind, fire, and earth—in a pseudoindigenous style with minimal reliance on Indian themes. Chávez described *Horsepower* as "a symphony of sounds around us, a revue of our times."[15] In style it is geometric machine music in the vein of Honegger's *Pacific 231* (1923), but contrasts the age of the machine with the Mexican life it affects. Part of the music of *Horsepower*—"La Danza de los Hombres y las Machinas" (The Dance of the Men and the Machines)—was presented in concert by the International Composers' Guild in New York's Aeolian Hall with Eugene Goosens conducting on November 28, 1926. This performance marked the first exposure of Chávez's orchestral music to audiences outside of Mexico.

The Symphony Orchestra of Mexico

When Chávez came back from New York in July, 1928, he was offered a proposition by the Sindicato de Músicos (Musicians' Union) to reorganize and conduct an orchestra called the Orquesta Sinfónica Mexicana (Mexican Symphony Orchestra) which had failed in its initial 1927–28 season after only three concerts. This failure was not unusual; of the several Mexican orchestras organized since the turn of the century, none had achieved lasting success, due partly to the political instability in the country. Moreover, the repertories of these orchestras had been limited mostly to conservative lyrical works and symphonic cycles (García Morillo, 57).

Foundation

The leadership of the musicians' union was at that time in the hands of the "jazzistas," many of whom Chávez knew from his engagement as an organist at the Olimpia theater in the 1925–26 season.[16] These musicians had been put out of work by the introduction of sound to motion pictures. They wanted to establish a permanent orchestra and wanted someone they had confidence in to conduct it. When Chávez was invited to be the musical director, he accepted their offer and mounted the first season of monthly concerts between September, 1928, and March, 1929. At the first meeting with the players he told them "We come to work and we aim for perfection. If we start seriously we will be recognized. We do not want to become just another orchestra."[17] The old name, Mexican Symphony Orchestra, was retained during the first season but was changed permanently to the Symphony Orchestra of Mexico (Orquesta Sinfónica de México) the following year.

Early Obstacles

There were serious artistic and economic problems to face at the outset, not to mention an indifferent public and a reactionary and hostile press. Chávez was able to fuse the "jazz" and "classical" factions and to overcome other difficulties in building a solid musical ensemble. Robert Stevenson has described some of the means with which Chávez was able to make his venture work.

[He] succeeded in building the first stable orchestra in Mexico in large measure because he knew how to win government as well as private support for his enterprise. He showed from the start his disposition to make his orchestra a national institution . . . unlike other conductors. he played all the orchestral works of young Mexican composers he could lay his hands on. He furthermore gave Mexican performing artists ample opportunities to be heard.

Stevenson cites an incident during the orchestra's first season that shows how Chávez could turn adverse criticism to his advantage. Blistering press notices followed the orchestra's performance of John Alden Carpenter's mechanistic and dissonant *Skyscraper Suite* on the second concert of the opening season in the Iris theater, October 7, 1929. An ongoing rankling in the press over this performance aroused public attention to the point that, when the same piece was repeated later in the season "by popular request," the performance was sold out.[18]

Building Audiences

The orchestra played in small halls at first (those seating 100–200 persons), but gradually outgrew them and moved into larger houses. On September 29, 1934, the orchestra moved into the newly completed Palacio de Bellas Artes (Palace of Fine Arts) which had been begun as the National Theatre in the Porfirio Díaz regime. Concerts were given to workers in parks and union headquarters, to children, to regular subscribers, and to ticket buyers. In regard to the workers' concerts, Chávez made these comments in his article "Music in a Mexican Test Tube" (*New York Times Magazine*, July 2, 1939).

[We] turned to the workers to create a new mass audience but didn't play down to them; they received the same fare as the regular Friday night subscription audiences . . . they liked Beethoven. Wagner. Rimsky-Korsakov. and Stravinsky and applauded spontaneously . . . When they didn't like something [for example. Haydn]. the silence was stoney . . . we are building a well educated audience in our land. an audience that cuts through all social strata.

The orchestra gave its first concert outside of Mexico City in 1941—at Puebla. In the following five seasons, the orchestra played in nineteen Mexican cities, in some of them repeatedly, and once in El Paso, Texas (in 1944). Also in 1944, the Mutual Radio Network carried the orchestra's Sunday evening concerts every week in a special series of summer broadcasts.

During its twenty-one years of operation, the orchestra continued to lengthen its seasons, to enlarge its list of Mexican and international guest conductors and soloists, and to introduce new music to Mexican audiences and to the world. In 1946, when he anticipated being appointed director of the National Institute of Fine Arts, Chávez named José Pablo Moncayo artistic director. Silvestre Revueltas had served as the assistant conductor from 1929 to 1935, and Eduardo Hernández Moncada from 1935 to 1945. Moncayo and especially Hernández Moncada remained close musical associates of Chávez in later years.

Repertory

In twenty-one seasons the orchestra played a total of 487 works of which 284 were Mexican premieres and eighty-eight world premieres. The formidable amount of new music was balanced with literature from the standard repertoire. Cycles of works, such as Beethoven's nine symphonies (for which Chávez was acknowledged as a leading interpreter), the fourth, fifth, and sixth symphonies of Tchaikowsky, Brahms's four symphonies, and the six *Brandenburg Concertos* by Bach, could be expected regularly. There were few gaps in the literature covered. However, as José Antonio Álcaraz has pointed out in his analysis of the orchestra's programming, the modern Viennese school was only minimally tapped; the two

Schoenberg works performed—*Verklärte Nacht* and *Five Pieces for Orchestra*—were from his early (pre-twelve-tone) period, and an orchestral rendering of excerpts from Berg's opera *Lulu* was the only other example included. Webern was completely passed over.[19] Virgil Thomson was so impressed with how much the balanced, and diversified repertory of the 1938–39 season said about the musical public in Mexico that he reprinted the entire program of six regular concerts, and the workers' and childrens' concerts without further comment in the *New York Herald Tribune*, March 16, 1941. By the 1940s, the orchestra had become a reason to visit Mexico.[20] At times, as much as an estimated one-fifth of the audience was from the United States. Lists of soloists, conductors, repertory, players, etc., for the Symphony Orchestra of Mexico appear in a book published by the orchestra entitled *21 Años de la Orquesta Sinfónica de México, 1928–1948* (Mexico City, 1948).[21]

National Conservatory and Department of Fine Arts

In December of 1928, Chávez was appointed director of the National Conservatory of Music by the new rector of the University, Antonio Castro Leal, replacing Carlos del Castillo. He occupied that post until March of 1933, and again from May to December of 1934. In the interim he served as chief of the Department of Fine Arts in the Secretariat of Public Education. There was opposition and resentment in some quarters to the selection of Chávez as head of the conservatory. Shortly after the public announcement was made, President Emilio Portes Gil called in the rector and showed him some 100 telegrams opposing Chávez's appointment, unproven as he was to manage such an important national institution. To Castro Leal's credit he stayed with his choice.[22] It was a wise and courageous decision.

The ninety-one-year-old conservatory was a staid, outmoded academic institution when the new director assumed authority. It was lacking in organization, and was almost completely devoid of a practical approach to the teaching of professional musicians. Chávez managed to have its dependency transferred from the university to the Secretariat of Public Education. There was a wholesale restructuring of the curriculum, young progressive teachers were hired, and promising student artists were given opportunities to perform at the regular conservatory concerts and, when merited, with his own Symphony Orchestra of Mexico. Chávez founded the important choral ensemble of the conservatory which he later turned over to one of his young faculty members, Luis Sandi. Some of the new faculty created a music journal called *Música, Revista Mexicana*

[Music, a Mexican Review]. The founders in addition to Chávez were Daniel Castañeda, Jerónimo Baqueiro Foster, Vincente T. Mendoza, Eduardo Hernández Moncada, Jesús C. Romero, José Pomar, David Saloma, José Rolón, and Luis Sandi.[23] Chávez, who saw to the promotion of his musical crusade with every available means, would not overlook such a ripe possibility for greater coverage in the press.

Composition Instruction

It was with composition teaching that the most sweeping changes were made. This might be expected of a self-taught composer who came to his new position with a strong bias against formalized instruction in his craft. Chávez faced the same tradition-bound methods of teaching composition in the conservatory which have been described earlier. In 1931 he instituted a new course in free composition with the approval of the Secretariat of Public Education. There was precedent for this free approach to expression in the plastic arts in the so-called Open Air Schools of Painting and the School of Sculpture and Direct Cutting (elimination of preliminary modelling in clay); however, the difference was that the conservatory was training professionals while the other schools mentioned provided only an introduction to creativity in the arts.

Chávez's pupils in the new composition class (called, at first, Class of Musical Creation and later, Composition Workshop) included some older members, notably Vincente Mendoza, Candelario Huizar, and Silvestre Revueltas. There were four students under twenty years of age: Daniel Ayala and Blas Galindo (both pure-blooded Indians), Salvador Contreras, and José Pablo Moncayo. In a 1936 article entitled "Revolt in Mexico" Chávez described the procedures he followed.

We used no text. All the students worked untiringly, writing melodies in all the diatonic modes, in a melodic scale of twelve tones, and in all of the pentatonic scales. Hundreds of melodies were written, but not merely as exercises on paper. We had instruments in the classroom, and the melodies were played on them, and found to be adequate or inadequate to the resources of the specific instruments. The result is that the young boys in particular now write melodies with amazingly acute instrumental feeling.

He adds that these young students went on to discover combining two and three melodies into a contrapuntal texture out of their own feeling of need for greater richness of sound.[24]

Academy of Investigation

An important new division of the conservatory was the Academy of Investigation. It was divided into three parts: I. Popular Music; II. History and Bibliography; and III. Investigation of New Musical Possibilities. Charged with the collecting of indigenous music (of category I) and the cataloging of it (category II), the academy had a very direct effect on Chávez's composition class. These investigations put into the hands of musicians and music students indigenous music and musical instruments hitherto unavailable to them in modern Mexico. The melodies unearthed by the academy were arranged by members of the composition class for a newly formed ensemble called the Mexican Orchestra which consisted of a mixture of modern orchestral instruments and Indian instruments. But the greatest value of the investigations to the composers was that they received "a living comprehension of the musical tradition of their own country."[25]

Success and Frustration in the Conservatory

The composition pupils began the historical portion of their studies with Chávez in 1933, but his departure from the conservatory the same year caused a hiatus in this part of their training. The students continued to study and write, however, and to achieve success as composers. The young four became known as Los Cuatro (The Four), an epithet after the model of The Mighty Five nineteenth-century Russian composers and Les Six, the French post-Impressionists. The only pupil of the class who did not succeed as a composer was Mendoza (who went on to an active career in music scholarship and criticism). This was due, according to Chávez, to the "stultifying effects of the academic instruction" he had undergone earlier.

In a lecture at Harvard University, where he held the Charles Eliot Norton poetic chair in 1958–59, Chávez described part of his mission at the conservatory and the partial frustration of his efforts caused by his departure from it in 1934.

Among [the problems I faced as director] was the idea of writing simple, melodic music with a peculiar Mexican flavor that would have a certain dignity and nobility of style; music that would be within the reach of the great mass of people . . . This plan included the foundation of choral groups . . . and the contributions of composers . . . As the project was beginning to take shape, I left the conservatory (late 1934) and there was nothing [more] anyone could do without the backing of the national institution.[26]

Department of Fine Arts

As chief of the Department of Fine Arts, Chávez was able to carry on some of the work begun in the Academy of Investigation at the conservatory, namely, collecting and cataloging native music, and the gathering and study of native instruments. The department also published a definitive book by Mendoza and Castañeda on the musical instruments of pre-conquest Mexico. Newly developed school choruses were taught to sing indigenous music, and the school children were treated to concerts of simple classical selections. Related programs were developed for dance and the plastic arts. These programs extended into special institutions such as the art schools for workers and the children's theater.[27] Chávez remained in the Department of Fine Arts from March, 1933, until May, 1934. Lázaro Cárdenas became president in 1934, and Chávez left the implementation of the new regime's "leftist policies" to his successor, Muñoz Cota.[28]

In managing three important positions in the early 1930s—director of a symphony orchestra and a national conservatory, and head of a multifaceted federal bureau—he was constantly in the public eye. That these activities also reaped financial success is revealed in his acquisition, in 1933, of a home in the elegant Las Lomas de Chapultepec district of Mexico City.

Mexican Nationalism and North American Recognition

If the period before 1934 was one of great growth for Chávez, the following few years represented fulfillment and recognition of that growth. His composing, conducting, and writings about music all gained towering respect in Mexico and the United States. His improved professional status in New York is reflected in the fact that he began staying in the Barbizon Plaza Hotel on Central Park South (one of his *Ten Preludes* for piano was written on the hotel's stationery in 1937). Compositions of this period show an intense nationalism enriched by the investigations into indigenous music he had initiated in the National Conservatory and the Department of Fine Arts.

More than half of Chávez's compositions written between 1932 and 1940 are nationalistic by virtue of either their subject matter, musical materials, instrumentation, or literary texts, or a combination of these elements. Two of these works *Sinfonía índia* (1935), employing Mexican Indian themes, and *El Sol* (1934), based on a ballad from the Mexican Revolution, soon gained popular acceptance in the United States. *Sinfonía índia*, written in New York, was premiered on CBS radio on January 23, 1936, with the composer conducting the CBS Symphony Orchestra.

Other nationalistic works of this period are *Cantos de México* [Songs of Mexico, 1933] for Mexican orchestra and chorus, *Llamadas* [Calls, 1934] for chorus and orchestra, and *Chapultepec* (1935), which presents three well-known songs from the revolution: "Zacatecas," "Club Verde," and "La Adelita." The poetry he set for either solo voice(s) or chorus during this period was exclusively Mexican, and four out of the five poets were his own contemporaries: Carlos Gutiérrez Cruz, Carlos Pellicer, Salvador Novo, and Xavier Villaurrutia.

Attention was showered on Mexican culture in 1940 in the form of an exposition at the Museum of Modern Art in New York City entitled "Twenty

Centuries of Mexican Art." Carlos Chávez, by then an established artist in New York, was asked by Nelson Rockefeller to organize a series of concerts of Mexican music to complement the exhibit. Rockefeller, who was then coordinator of the Office of Inter-American Affairs for the U. S. State Department, was serving as vice-chairman of the board of directors at the museum, and had been named to direct this auspicious exhibit.

The concerts combined music from several regions of Mexico and from historical periods covering antiquity, colonialism, and the revolution. Chávez and his associates, including former conservatory students Galindo, Huizar, and Mendoza, arranged the music for indigenous instruments brought from Mexico. For his part, Chávez composed *Xochipilli, an Imagined Aztec Music* (1940) and arranged *La Paloma Azul* [The Blue Dove, 1940] for chorus and orchestra. His earlier *Chapultepec* and two dances from the 1926 ballet *Los Cuatro Soles* were also included on the programs. Columbia Records commemorated the concerts with a sumptuous record album of the music performed in the museum concerts (Columbia ML 2080).

Chávez was a true nationalist; however, as Herbert Weinstock has written, he was not a nationalist in "any jingoistic sense, but as one who feels close to his land and its people, who finds their music in his own memory . . ."[29]

Away from Nationalism

Not all of Chávez's creative energy was directed toward nationalism during the thirties. He was also striking out in new directions with absolute and abstract music which had no identifiable connection with Mexico beyond a few idiosyncrasies of rhythm and melody which had already become part of his working vocabulary.

A new practice originating from the 1930s was Chávez's adaptation of other composers' music for his own use. For example, he orchestrated Buxtehude's *Chaconne in E minor* (1937), leaving intact the original musical content but cloaking it in modern orchestral colors. In his *Trio* (1940), he arranged piano music and piano/vocal music by Debussy and Falla for flute, harp, and viola. A method he used often in later works stems from his *Soli I* for oboe, clarinet, bassoon, and trumpet (1933). In this work, which he composed at the request of the League of Composers for its tenth anniversary celebration, he employed a "nonrepetitive technique" in which each new musical idea in its turn becomes an antecedent to the next consequent idea in a constant renewal of invention.

Two of Chávez's most important nonnationalistic compositions of the period under discussion are his *Sinfonía de Antígona* (1933), which grew out of incidental music he wrote for a Jean Cocteau version of the Sophocles play presented in Mexico in 1932, and his duo for violin and piano entitled *Three*

Spirals (1934). Elliott Carter praised these works in 1937 as having been "conceived in a new idiom transforming musical speech to its own ends."[30] *Three Spirals* was premiered by Joseph Szigetti in a Town Hall recital January 30, 1937.

The Written Word

From his youth Chávez had found the written word an effective vehicle for promoting the causes he wished to advance and for articulating his methods of advancing them. His writing reflects an inquisitive, energetic, and assertive mind with a sense of history which he used as a rudder to steer the forward course of his musical thinking. In his article "The Two Persons," appearing in the *Musical Quarterly* in 1929,[31] he delineated the responsibility of the performing musician to observe with the greatest fidelity the directions given by the composer. He acknowledged the unique danger in music, in contrast to painting, sculpture, and architecture, of having a work of art reach the consumer in a form other than what the artist created.

A trip to Philadelphia in 1932 led to Chávez's next major monograph on music. He was there for the world premiere of his ballet *Horsepower* (March 31) conducted by Leopold Stokowski. Stokowski, who had conducted Chávez's orchestra in Mexico in 1931, was perhaps reciprocating his Mexican colleague's hospitality when he took the young composer to visit the R.C.A. Victor studios in Camden, New Jersey, and the Bell Telephone Laboratories in New York. Chávez had been commissioned by the Secretary of Public Education in Mexico to report on the latest musical developments in the United States. His report, serialized in the Mexico City daily *El Universal* in July and August of 1932, was mainly a commentary on the advanced state of development in electronics and the benefits which were accruing to or could accrue to the art of music. These newspaper accounts became the genesis of his book *Toward a New Music*, which appeared in 1937.[32]

In *Toward a New Music*, Chávez was as abreast of reality as he was in his *Horsepower* ballet. He predicted practical uses of the new developing technology which have since materialized in compositions making use of the manipulation and superimposition of recorded sound. His vision of a future for electronics within the realm of serious music has been realized on a large scale within the last two decades with the sophistication and mass production of music synthesizers which greatly augment the range of sound resources.

Conducting: United States Debut

Chávez's growing reputation as a conductor brought him invitations for guest appearances with orchestras in several major U.S. cities between 1936 and 1940;

these included New York, Philadelphia, Pittsburgh, Cleveland, Washington, Los Angeles, San Francisco, and St. Louis. As already noted, he conducted the CBS radio orchestra for the *Sinfonía India* premiere in 1936. In March of 1938 he was called on by NBC to conduct a series of weekly radio concerts after Arturo Toscanini's sudden departure. The players quickly became acquainted with his thoroughness when he rehearsed Ravel's *Bolero* for over two hours.[33]

On the occasion of his debut with the New York Philharmonic, February 11, 1937, Chávez drew unanimous praise from the New York critics, some comparing him favorably with Toscanini.[34] Chávez was one of three illustrious composer-conductors (the other two: Igor Stravinsky and Georges Enesco) engaged by the New York Philharmonic for the 1936–37 season in answer to allegations that the orchestra was neglecting contemporary music.[35] Another prestigious conducting appearance occurred on April 10, 1937, when Chávez directed the orchestra at the Eighth Festival of Chamber Music, sponsored by the Elizabeth Sprague Coolidge Foundation at the Library of Congress in Washington, D.C. He led the ensemble in a performance of the first two movements of his *Concerto for Four Horns* (1937–38) and Paul Hindemith's *Der Schwandrehrer* with the German composer playing the solo viola part in his American debut.[36]

Though his success as a conductor continued to grow throughout his long career, it never obscured the fact that he considered himself first and foremost a composer. Explaining this attitude, he wrote that his activities in education, administration, writing and conducting "have had no other sense than to provide a larger field as a composer."[37] Indeed the "field" was growing on an international scale. Nicolas Slonimsky conducted the world premiere of his *Energía* at the second annual Pan-American Concert in Paris on June 11, 1931.

Maturity and Universalism

In 1938 Chávez received a John Simon Guggenheim grant to compose his *Concerto for Piano with Orchestra*. The concerto received its premiere January 1, 1942, with Dimitri Mitropoulis conducting the New York Philharmonic, and Eugene List as soloist. The word "with" in the title is significant: the piano is treated as an integral part of the orchestra.[38] The work combines a synthesis of Indian melodic and rhythmic materials with an international personal style which transcends nationalism. Otto Meyer-Serra has called it a universal work due to the personalization of folk elements.[39] Not everyone liked the *Concerto*, but those who heard it were aware of a profound musical statement and the strong personal stamp of its composer. With this composition a new plateau of maturity was reached.

In the late 1930s, Chávez was asked by John Cage to write a piece for his percussion ensemble in Chicago. He complied with the *Toccata for Percussion* (1942), but Cage's group was unable to play it;[40] its initial performance took place in Mexico City at the hands of the percussion section of Chávez's orchestra in 1947. Since its publication in 1954, the piece has become a regular feature of both student and professional percussion ensemble programs on three continents. It demonstrates how Chávez could turn a commission of seemingly modest proportions into a work of major artistic significance.

Chávez turned to ballet again in 1943 with a commission from the Elizabeth Sprague Coolidge Foundation for a work to be choreographed by Martha Graham and to be danced by her troupe. This ballet, the composer's first since *Horsepower* in 1926, avoided any Indian orientation. It is more akin to his *Sinfonía Antígona* (1933) with its basis in Greek mythology. Its first title, *La Hija de Cólquide* [The Daughter of Colchis] was changed to *Dark Meadow* and its plot drastically altered for the 1946 New York premiere. The ballet, originally for a double quartet of string and woodwinds, was also arranged by the composer as a symphonic suite employing five of its original sections. Three of its other sections were extracted to constitute the *Cuarteto de Arcos III* [String Quartet No. 3]. As with *Horsepower*, appropriation of concert music from the original dramatic context made *La Hija de Cólquide* considerably more serviceable.

Texts of songs and choral settings show a broader base of poetic sources during the period of the early forties than earlier. The text of Chávez's first music written for a capella chorus, *Arbolucu, te sequeste* [Tree of Sorrow, 1942], was taken from a traditional Spanish song. His *Three Nocturnes* (1942) were composed to poems of nineteenth-century English romantic poets Keats, Shelley, and Byron. In other works he used anonymous fifteenth-century poetry (*A Woman is a Worthy Thing*, 1942), a poem from the fourteenth century by John Barbour (*A! Freedome*, 1942), and traditional songs from Ecuador (*Cuatro Melodias Tradicionales Índias del Ecuador*, 1942). But Mexican poets—Villaurrutia (*North Carolina Blues*, 1942) and Enrique Gonzales Martínez (*Canto a la Tierra*, 1946)—were not overlooked.

Colegio Nacional

A national distinction was bestowed on Carlos Chávez in 1943 when he became one of thirteen charter members of the Colegio Nacional (National College) along with painters Diego Rivera and José Orozco and several prominent Mexican writers and scientists. The College sponsored each of its members in public lectures annually and made the texts of selected lectures available in printed form.

Chávez changed the format of his presentations from lecture to lecture-concert after 1949, continuing almost every year through 1976. He covered a wide range of topics from "Jazz" to "Vivaldi" to "Composers of the Avant-Garde in Mexico," illustrating his points at the piano, and employing guest soloists.[41]

Ediciones Mexicanas de Música

In 1945, Chávez met in Mexico City with several Mexican and expatriate Spanish composers to consider a cooperative association to publish their music. The idea may have come from the quarterly publication *New Music* in San Francisco which printed a large quantity of modern music in the 1930s including Chávez's *Spiral* in 1935 and *Seven Pieces for Piano* in 1936. In 1946, Chávez was able to get government financial support for the project, and increased the support when he became Director of the National Institute of Fine Arts (INBA) in 1947. Thus began the organization known as Ediciones Mexicanas de Música which still continues its publishing operation in Mexico. Chávez's *La Casada Infiel* [The Faithless Wife], *Estudio a Chopin* in 1946, and *Canto a la Tiérra* were published by Ediciones (in 1960, 1949, and 1946 respectively).

The same Mexican and Spanish composers joined with Chávez in 1946 to establish a music periodical as the journal of Ediciones Mexicanas. Rodolfo Halffter became the editor of the new periodical, *Nuestra Música*, and the editorial board included Jesús Bal y Gay, Blas Galindo, José Pablo Moncayo, Adolfo Salazar, Luis Sandi, and Chávez. Their common desire was "to contribute to the musical development of Mexico through the focusing of attention on their national achievement."[42] The first issue had articles by Chávez, Bartók, and Salazar. Chávez's detailed series entitled "Initiation to Orchestral Direction" was printed in *Nuestra Música* in four issues from 1946 to 1948 (nos. 4, 5, 6, and 9).

It may have been more than by coincidence that *Nuestra Música* began publishing in the same year that the periodical *Modern Music*, the official organ of the League of Composers, ended its twenty-three years of spokesmanship for contemporary music. Chávez knew *Modern Music* well; he had contributed to it and was often reviewed in its pages by other composers and critics; in fact, since its first mention of him in 1928, *Modern Music* carried some reference to Chávez in all but two of its quarterly issues through 1946.[43] *Nuestra Música* continued publishing in quarterly editions through 1949, and in three installments per year thereafter through 1952.

The same group of composers inaugurated a series of "Monday Concerts" with the primary purpose of promoting their own music. It was their belief that the concerts would provide new and unique opportunities for performing musicians and cultivate audiences in a milieu of living and growing sonorous art.

National Institute of Fine Arts

Miguel Alemán in his campaign for the Mexican presidency announced his intention to create a new institution which would support and govern the activities of art and literature at the national level. Carlos Chávez, probably the artist with the greatest visibility in Mexico at the time, was called upon in 1945 to direct the Commission of the National Alemán Committee in developing a plan for such an institution. After deliberations concerning purview, structure, and implementation, a plan was reached in early 1946. Alemán was, of course, elected president; the plan was written into law on December 31, 1946. On January 1, 1947, The National Institute of Fine Arts and Literature began operation with Chávez as its director general.

The institute was structured as a branch of the Secretariat of Public Education and was answerable to it. But in actuality the institute's charter, drawn up by Chávez under the most favorable political circumstances, gave it a sweeping autonomy that afforded almost exclusive authority in the arts.[44]

The institute consisted of six departments: Music, Dance, Theater, Architecture, and Administration. Soon afterward, in March of 1947, structural modifications were made to accommodate practical needs: a Consulting Technical Council and a Council of Pedagogic Technique were added; the Department of Theater added literature, and a new Department of Theatrical Production was instituted; a new periodical, *Mexico en el Arte* [Mexico in Art], was authorized; and an editorial department created. Chávez's disciples Sandi and Galindo were appointed respectively sub-director of the institute and head of the Department of Music. Chávez named himself Provisional Director of the Department of Dance (García Morillo, 129f).

The amount of organization required to manage so large, multifaceted, and far-reaching a conglomerate was enormous. Alemán, while honoring Chávez for his record of artistic achievement in Mexico, had to be aware of his proven organizational ability. It was not a bad political liaison for Alemán to cultivate either. In 1951, Luis Sandi called Chávez "the most important musician in Mexico in the past fifty years," adding that it was his extraordinary talent for administration and organization which brought success to him and to those he represented.[45]

The first year of the institute produced results exceeding all expectations. There were expositions, "the most superb in the immediate present in the world, Mexican ballet, theater, and an invisible but effective teaching tool that was extending in all directions to the general public."[46]

End of the Symphony Orchestra of Mexico

With all of his new and increasing responsibility in the Institute of Fine Arts, Chávez still held the titular directorship of the Symphony Orchestra of Mexico. Actually, he was still serving as the musical director. As has been pointed out, Chávez felt that his first commitment was as a composer, and he was finding too little time to compose. On January 19, 1949, he presented a letter of resignation to the managing council of the orchestra. In that letter, he reminded the council that he had resigned four years earlier (June 23, 1945) but was persuaded to stay on as titular director, with the hope of improvement in the orchestra's administrative structure.

The hoped for administrative improvement did not materialize, but he said that even if it had, he felt compelled to dedicate himself "exclusively and with complete concentration to composition and study." The managing council replied on March 8, 1949, that his resignation had been accepted, but that the orchestra was dissolved by revocation of the civil association by which it had been officially chartered in 1940. The reason given was that the "Symphony Orchestra of Mexico was in reality, the personal work of Carlos Chávez who founded it in 1928 and directed it uninterruptedly for twenty-one seasons" (García Morillo, 145ff).

Birth of the National Symphony Orchestra

Chávez had already formed a new orchestra within the Institute of Fine Arts nearly two years earlier on July 10, 1947—the Orquesta Sinfónica Nacional del Conservatorio (National Symphony Orchestra of the Conservatory). In 1948 he offered José Pablo Moncayo, who had been his "official" musical director in the last few seasons with the Symphony Orchestra of Mexico, four pairs of concerts to conduct that season. Chávez believed this would give Moncayo the opportunity he needed to be free from his (Chávez's) shadow; Moncayo turned the offer down.[47] Eduardo Hernández Moncada became the first director of the new orchestra, but, by its third year, the orchestra, which had dropped "of the Conservatory" from its title, enjoyed a healthy and successful season under none other than Moncayo.[48] In 1950, Chávez called the National Symphony a "continuation" of the Symphony Orchestra of Mexico "which was not national in its organization but was national in its orientation."[49] As could be expected, Chávez guest-conducted the National Symphony Orchestra often in the years following (through 1971).

Productivity in the Institute of Fine Arts

While he was still director (until 1952) of the Institute of Fine Arts, Chávez brought additional instrumental ensembles under its umbrella. To the National

Symphony Orchestra and the Gonzales and Contreras String Quartets were added the Fine Arts Chamber Orchestra, the Fine Arts Woodwind Quintet, and the Art Quartet. This thriving growth is also mirrored in the Department of Dance, which in Chávez's final two years at the Institute, presented thirty ballets, twenty-five of them by Mexican composers (García Morillo, 149f). The opera seasons radiated with brilliant stagings of European and Mexican works. Boito, Gluck, Monteverdi, and Humperdinck operas were complemented with new Mexican offerings by Moncayo, Hernández Moncada, and Sandi.[50]

Chávez's creative output during the institute years was limited in quantity as would be expected from the magnitude of his responsibility. However, some major works did emanate from that period. The *Violin Concerto*, begun in 1948, was completed in 1950; the Chopin-engendered piano studies were written in 1949 and 1950. Of these piano works, *Three Etudes for Piano, á Chopin* and *Estudio IV, Homenaje a Chopin* [Etude IV, Homage to Chopin], were commissioned by UNESCO in Paris to commemorate the centennial of Chopin's death. Chávez travelled to Paris for the occasion. The *Left Hand Inversions of Five Chopin Etudes* (1950) were inspired by Chopin but not written for the centennial.

The Symphonic Years

The years between 1953 and 1961 have been called with good reason the "symphonic years," since during that period Chávez wrote the last four of his six symphonies. But he did not limit himself to this single genre of composition. Two important dramatic compositions from the period are his only opera, *The Visitors*, and his cantata *Prometheus Bound*. Two progressive instrumental works from 1958 and 1961 respectively are *Invención* [Invention] for piano and *Soli II for Wind Quintet*. In addition to his composing, Chávez taught in the summer of 1953 at the Berkshire Music Festival in Tanglewood, Massachusetts, he was "Slee" Visiting Professor of Music at the University of Buffalo in 1958, and held the Charles Eliot Norton Poetic Chair at Harvard University in the 1958–59 academic year. He was honored for the second time by the Guggenheim Foundation with a grant for composition (for *Prometheus*) in 1956. Add to this a conducting schedule that took him to Europe, South America, Mexico, and many cities in the United States, and the sum reveals a highly diversified and productive nine-year period.

Symphonies III through VI

The symphonies 3 through 6 were all written on commissions. *Symphony No. 3*, composed for Clare Boothe Luce, was begun in 1951 but not completed until

1954. *Symphony No. 4* (1953), subtitled *Sinfónica Romántica* [Romantic Symphony], was commissioned by the Louisville Symphony, and The Serge Koussevitsky Foundation provided the commission for *Symphony No. 5* for strings.

In 1959, Chávez was invited as one of ten composers who would each write a new orchestra work for the opening of Philharmonic Hall in Lincoln Center. The composers, in addition to Chávez, were Samuel Barber, Leonard Bernstein, Aaron Copland, Alberto Ginastera, Werner Henze, Paul Hindemith, Darius Milhaud, Francis Poulenc, and William Schuman. Chávez's offering was his monumental *Symphony No. 6* which was eventually premiered at Philharmonic Hall (a year and one-half after the opening) on May 7, 1964, with Leonard Bernstein conducting.

His final four symphonies are all in the category of "absolute" music, that is, having no descriptive or otherwise extra-musical connections. They represent a more conservative outlook than other works from this period, especially *Invención* for piano (1958) and *Soli II for Wind Quintet* (1961). Maybe the composer felt he could be more daring and experimental with these last two works because they were not written at the behest of a benefactor.

Opera

Chávez had considered writing an opera since the early 1930s, but he did not find a libretto with the balance of reality and fantasy to please him until Chester Kallman's *The Tuscan Players*, written in 1953 (García Morillo, 171).

Chávez labored with the opera for four years, and it was finally staged in the Brander Matthews Theatre at Columbia University in New York in 1957 with the new title (the second of four) *Panfilo and Lauretta*. There was a last minute rush to prepare the orchestra parts. At the Second Interamerican Festival of Music in Caracas in 1957, several composers present assisted Chávez in copying parts from the score to help him meet the fast approaching production deadline.[51] Likewise Virgil Thomson and other friends assisted with the final copying in New York.[52] This work was to become one of Chávez's most troublesome creations, but one in which he believed strongly.[53]

Teaching and Lecturing: the 1950s

Chávez spent a few weeks at the Berkshire Music Festival in Tanglewood, Massachusetts, as guest professor of composition in the summer of 1953. One of his pupils that summer, Edward Miller, who later became a professor of composition at Oberlin College Conservatory of Music, had these observations to make about the maestro's teaching:

I remember his having us compose in the modes (three short woodwind quartets), and study the Beethoven 5th [Symphony], and one statement still sticks in my mind: "You must compose eight hours a day, study scores eight hours a day, and practice for the other eight hours."[54]

In the spring of 1958 Chávez gave a series of lectures at the University of Buffalo, following which, in the fall of 1958, he began a seven month tenure as recipient of the Charles Eliot Norton Poetic Chair at Harvard University. This distinguished teaching professorship, endowed in 1926, has been filled by a distinguished writer or musician each year since its founding. Among the illustrious writers have been Robert Frost, E. E. Cummings, and Octavio Paz. The musicians who preceded Chávez were Igor Stravinsky (1939–40), Paul Hindemith (1949–50), and Aaron Copland (1951–52).

Chávez's six lectures were eventually published in *Musical Thought* (Cambridge, Mass.: Harvard University Press, 1960). Topics included "A Latin American Composer," in which he surveys indigenous music resources; "Art as Communication," which stresses the need for composers to know the composition techniques of the past; and the "Composer and the Public," which deals with Ortega y Gasset's "period of quarantine" a composer must endure if he writes music that is ahead of its time. But perhaps his own personal credo of composition comes out best in the lecture entitled "The Enjoyment of Music":

A composer should know everything that has been done in composition before him: know it well and thoroughly. But he should not follow any rules in writing his music, because in music there are no general rules; there are only special rules, personal rules: Wagner's rules were good for Wagner, and Schoenberg's for Schoenberg.

He then cites Busoni's statement that "the function of the creative artist consists in making laws, not in following laws already made."[55]

The seven month stay in Cambridge was a fruitful period intellectually, musically (he made several conducting appearances while in the Boston area), and financially: Chávez told Nicolas Slonimsky that he was paid $21,000 for the six Norton lectures.[56]

The Bountiful Sixties

Chávez balanced a full schedule of conducting, teaching, and composing in the 1960s. During these years, his sphere of conducting activity extended deeply into Western Europe while he continued to accept invitations to conduct in the United States and Latin America. In 1960, he was appointed by Mexican President Adolfo López Mateos to establish the Taller de Creación Musical (Workshop of Musical Creation) in the National Conservatory, where he remained for four

years. His major commissions during this period were a work for the opening
of the National Museum of Archeology in Mexico—*Resonáncias* [Resonances,
1964], a piece for the third Interamerican Music Festival—*Invention No. 2*
(1965), *Elatio* [Elation, 1967] to commemorate the centennial of the restoration
of the Mexican Republic, and *Pirámide* [Pyramid, 1968] for the Mexican
Folkloric Ballet. These were rich and rewarding years in terms of creativity,
re-creative activity, and teaching.

Conducting: the 1960s

In 1962, Chávez made guest conducting appearances in Bergen (Norway),
Berlin, Río de Janeiro, Tel Aviv,[57] Mexico City, Seattle, Brussels, Paris, and
Vienna, and conducted the North German Radio Network Orchestra. Not since
leaving the Symphonic Orchestra of Mexico in 1948, had he channeled so much
of his energy into conducting. A reviewer for the *Los Angeles Herald Examiner*,
who attended a concert of the Los Angeles Philharmonic Chávez conducted on
July 26, 1966, praised his interpretation of Debussy's *La Mer*:

As often as this work has been performed it can seldom have received better treatment than
was accorded it last night at the hands of the Los Angeles Philharmonic, abetted by guest
conductor Carlos Chávez . . . So incisive was the beat and leadership of Chávez that not
one musical gaucherie of consequence escaped the [Hollywood Bowl] shell

His own reading of his *Symphony No. 5* with the Los Angeles Chamber Orchestra
on March 6, 1966, was reviewed in the *Los Angeles Times* as follows:

With Chávez on the podium, the composition was not only in the hands of its creator, but
also in those of a master conductor. From the outset they [the musicians] sat up and took
note of Chávez's commanding presence, delivering a performance that ended in cheers and
ovation.

From these and other critical reviews from the middle and later 1960s, it is
clear that Chávez had reached full maturity as a conductor.[58] His care in carrying
out composers' intentions, and his uncompromising standard of excellence had
always set him apart as an exceptional interpreter. But with these traits and a
musical acumen gained from experience, his conducting had now attained its
highest level.

Return to the National Conservatory

The composition workshop Mexican President Adolfo López Mateos authorized
through the Secretariat of Public Education in 1960 was soon renamed Taller de
Composición Carlos Chávez. It was developed as an instructional program for a
few of the most talented composition students in Mexico. Chávez, as director,
chose as his assistant Hernández Moncada. Soon afterward, Hernández Moncada

was succeeded by Spanish-born Cuban composer Julián Orbón, whom Chávez had met at the First Festival of Latinamerican Music in Caracas in 1954. The seven students initially accepted into the workshop were Jorgé Daher, Humberto Hernández Medrano, Eduardo Mata, Hector Quintanar, Jesús Villaseñor, Julio Estrada, and Leonardo Velásquez (the last two remained only a few weeks). Orbón, who moved to New York in 1963, has continued to employ the composition teaching techniques he acquired at the workshop. He described the method Chávez used as follows:

The students were assigned a particular Mozart sonata which they analyzed harmonically and motivically. Then they wrote a piece of identical length, on the same harmony, and with the same number and character of motives. [Witness Chávez's *Sonata No. 5* (1960) on a harmonic scheme of Mozart *Sonata K. 533/594.*] The piece was performed, criticized, and then a free composition in the same style was assigned. It was also performed and evaluated. This process was repeated by each student after models of a Beethoven string quartet, a Schubert song, a Chopin piano piece, and works by Strauss and Debussy.[59]

Pianist María Teresa Rodríguez, who was engaged to assist in performing the students' works for solo piano and voice and piano, attests to the musical insight she as well as the students received in this rarified atmosphere.[60]

It may be revealing to look at a typical day in the composition workshop and some of the maestro's direction of it as recalled by Hernández Medrano.

The students arrived early in the morning to develop their incipient compositions. Each had his own studio, and each studio could be and was observed by Chávez from a central vantage point. At 4:00 P.M., we would gather with the maestro to revise the work of the day before. His criticisms and comments were objective and exacting but deeply respectful of the students' points of view. This was followed by an analysis of the classics. He employed a concept in harmonic analysis of floating chromaticism, and in structural analysis, a proportional system of such efficacy that the most abstruse and complex score was revealed before our eyes as a sonorous architecture of simple and accessible profiles. Performance of the student works [by professional musicians] followed, and Chávez would respond to them with comments of a more general nature. The day's work usually ended about 8:00 P.M.[61]

A major benefit of this unique system of instruction was that the students heard their works immediately after they wrote them, performed by professional artists. Soprano Irma González sang the songs each student wrote; the Ferrari String Quartet—Franco Ferrari, Manuel Enríques, Gilberto García, and Adolfo Odnopossoff (later, Sally van den Berg)—played their string quartets. The Fine Arts Opera Orchestra read their orchestral pieces and on one occasion performed symphonies by Mata, Hernández Medrano, and Quintanar in the Palace of Fine Arts. They used Brahms's four symphonies and *Violin Concerto* as their orchestral models in the procedure described by Orbón above. Chávez's own *Sixth*

Symphony, composed in 1960 and 1961, conspicuously employs a passacaglia set of variations in its final movement as does the Brahms *Fourth Symphony.*

President López Mateos visited the workshop and took particular pride in its concept and progress; Aaron Copland also paid visits when in Mexico. Chávez left the workshop in 1964 after seeing the first class of students through; he named alumnus Hector Quintanar the new director.

Of the five students who completed the workshop under Chávez's direction, two have followed conducting careers: Mata at Phoenix (until 1977) and Dallas as musical director, and as permanent guest conductor of the London Symphony Orchestra; Quintanar, who established the first electronic music studio in Mexico with Chávez's sponsorship, later directed the Orchestra of the National Free University of Mexico (a position previously held by Mata). Hernández Medrano heads his own Workshop of Polyphonic Studies in Mexico City; he also teaches at the National Conservatory as does Villaseñor. Daher is the only one of the five who did not pursue music as a profession.[62]

Composition: the 1960s

According to Orbón, Chávez's abstract (nonnationalistic music) developed along two tracks throughout his career: first, the traditional, culminating in his *Symphony No. 6;* and second, the experimental—*Solis, Inventions,* and his orchestral works from the 1960s. Originating from this period are the "experimental" works *Soli III* and *Soli IV* (1965 and 1966), *Inventions Nos. 2* and *3* (1965 and 1967), *Resonances* (1964) *Pyramid* (1968), and *Discovery* (1969). A tribute to the more traditional side of his output came about with the Columbia recording (3230064) of his six symphonies in 1966. This recording, commissioned by the Secretariat of Public Education and carried out with Chávez conducting the National Symphony Orchestra of Mexico, was awarded the Koussevitzky International Prize in 1968.[63]

The decade of the sixties ended in sadness for Chávez when his daughter Juanita died in October, 1969, from complications following surgery. Those close to the composer say the trauma of this personal loss impaired his work for several months. (He did not complete a single composition in 1970.)

The Lyre of Orpheus

In January of 1969, Chávez wrote an essay (or lecture) entitled the "Lyre of Orpheus" in which he sharply criticized the declining state of music in Mexico. A typescript of this brief monologue remains among the memorabilia to the composer in the archive of CENIDIM: Centro National de Investigación, Documentación, e Información Musical Carlos Chávez (Carlos Chávez National Center of

Musical Research, Documentation, and Information).[64] He answers his rhetorical question, "what are the guardians of culture going to do?" with this response:

I don't know, but one thing is certain: they would be able, if they so desire, to take the lyre of Orpheus into their own hands: to spread the good art wherever they wish and to capture the souls, even the most calloused among them. To carry to everyone the high art that dignifies and elevates.

Here is Chávez not in any official position to carry the "Lyre of Orpheus" as he had done for so long in Mexico. In the Conservatory, in the Department of Fine Arts, with the Symphony Orchestra of Mexico, in the Institute of Fine Arts, and in the Composition Workshop he was able to bear that legendary symbol of music and invoke its powers to elevate, dignify, and "capture the souls" of his countrymen. His latest withdrawal from the leadership of Mexican musical life was a consequence of his own need for more time to create, to compose; that had always been his first calling. Nevertheless, he could not ignore, at this juncture the fact that no one was carrying the torch, there was no one "taking the lyre of Orpheus" into his own hands.

"National Plan" for Music

President Luis Echeverría was either aware of the plight of serious music in Mexico, or was made aware of it when he appointed Chávez as his advisor in 1971. He charged Chávez with the responsibility to develop a "national plan" for music which would get to the root level with music instruction for all elementary school students.[65] Chávez had criticized the conservatory for its poor teachers, and the National Symphony Orchestra for its mediocre directors and for having essentially the same repertory as when he left it.[66] His "national plan" would no doubt include measures to correct these deficiencies as well.

Chávez was to begin implementing the "national plan" on December 23, 1972, according to an article in *El Heraldo* (December 13). On January 3, 1973, came the announcement of his appointment as head of the Department of Music in The National Institute of Fine Arts, and director of the National Symphony Orchestra. The notice of his double appointment carried more details of the national plan"—measures "which will include improvement of the National Symphony Orchestra, the National Opera Company, and the Fine Arts Chamber Orchestra." He planned some 200 concerts for the National Orchestra from February to December and a seven week tour of the provinces.[67] Chávez also announced several key appointments to various music organizations: Eduardo Hernández Moncada, director of the Opera Orchestra with Hector Quintanar as his assistant; and Imre Hartman and Fernando Lozano as codirectors of the Fine Arts Chamber Orchestra.[68]

The National Symphony Fiasco

A number of Mexican musicians who had left Mexico for careers elsewhere made plans to return to play in the National Symphony when they learned Chávez was to be its director.[69] But there was trouble ahead at the National Symphony Orchestra. Chávez had advertised auditions at the Juilliard School of Music in New York for fourteen orchestral positions in the National Symphony Orchestra and the Fine Arts Chamber Orchestra in Mexico City.[70] He engaged several musicians as a result of these auditions, and they appeared at the initial rehearsal of the National Symphony which he conducted. There was resentment at the displacement of Mexican musicians by the foreigners. But Chávez later explained, in *Excelsior*, March 5, 1973, the problem was more fundamental than that.

Four or five months before he took charge of the orchestra, the "orchestra commission" (comprised of elected orchestra members) had asked the Institute of Fine Arts to allow a council of equal representation from the orchestra and from the institute to decide on all matters determining its musical director, assistant and guest conductors, personnel, programs, seasons, etc. The institute, as Chávez understood it, had responded negatively to their proposal, but only verbally.

At the conclusion of the first rehearsal he conducted, Chávez was informed by the orchestra commission that it was "not going to relent on its claims for an equal voice in management," to which Chávez responded that he could not accept the directorship of an orchestra without having artistic control. At the second rehearsal, no one played at the downbeat. A strike of orchestra musicians ensued, instigated by the National Symphony Orchestra incidents, but drawing majority membership from other orchestras, including the Orchestra of the Free University, the Fine Arts Chamber Orchestra, and the Opera Orchestra. The musicians claimed Chávez was an illegally appointed orchestra director, and they criticized some of the appointments he was making (or was alleged to be making) in his capacity as head of the Department of Music.[71] Faced with an obvious lack of support from the president (who had appointed him), the Institute of Fine Arts, and the musicians, and with the flames of opposition fanned out of control, Chávez saw no alternative but to step down. He resigned both the directorship of the orchestra and of the Department of Music before the end of January, 1973.

Cabrillo Music Festival

Chávez's star was still rising on other horizons. After a successful performance of his orchestral piece, *Discovery*, at the Cabrillo Music Festival in Aptos, California, in the summer of 1969, he was invited to become musical director of the festival for the following season. The festival had experienced fading interest and lagging box office support in its previous few seasons. Chávez agreed to direct the 1970 festival season, but only on the condition that a "strictly professional orchestra" be hired. An agreement was reached, and he proceeded to recruit an orchestra through open auditions to supplement the nucleus of players drawn from the Oakland Symphony. The 1970 season consisted of seven concerts over two consecutive weekends.[72] Chávez was able to revitalize the festival both artistically, as the reviews bear out, and financially. He directed the festival for four successive seasons through 1973.

After the auditions for the 1971 season, Chávez announced that he could not hire an orchestra from San Francisco based on the auditions he heard. The situation was resolved by means of hiring a professional contractor who engaged some of the same musicians Chávez had rejected, showing that the maestro's idealism could be tempered with practicality when necessary.[73]

Teaching and Lecturing: the 1970s

The enthusiasm for teaching and musical involvement with students that Chávez revealed early in his career continued as a vital force in the later years. Between 1972 and 1975 he accepted invitations for lectures and conducting appearances from several colleges and universities in the United States and England, including New York University (1972), University of Durham, York University, and Northern University (1973), California State at Long Beach (1974), Louisiana State University, Peabody Conservatory, Indiana State University, and San Jose State (1975). His unrelenting responsibility to, and vigorous role in education, must be assessed as one of his most encompassing contributions to the musical art.

Composition: the 1970s

Chávez remained busy with composing and revising earlier works in the seventies. For the opening of the Edwin J. Thomas Performing Arts Hall at the University of Akron, he wrote *Initium* for orchestra. He recast his 1934 *Llamadas* for chorus and orchestra as an orchestral piece in 1973, retitled as *Paisajes Mexicanos* [Mexican Landscapes]. The Music Department of the National Free University of Mexico commissioned *Sonante* (1974) for string orchestra, and for the Arthur Rubinstein Israeli Festival he composed *Estudio a Rubinstein* [Etude to Rubinstein, 1973]. He added several short a cappella choral works, *Cinco Caprichos* for piano, a piece for solo guitar, one for solo timpani, a cello concerto (only partially completed), and his final major work, the *Concerto for Trombone and Orchestra* (1976).

Chávez's Composing Process

The mechanical procedure by which Chávez transmitted musical ideas to notation is not particularly unique. He preferred to compose at the piano, but seems to have been comfortable writing music when an instrument was not at hand. During brief stops in hotels, or when travelling by train or airplane, he composed without a piano. However, on extended stays, for example, at the Barbizon Plaza or at One Lincoln Plaza in New York, he would acquire an instrument. Julián Orbón and others affirm that Chávez did not have absolute pitch. But obviously he could formulate his musical imagery mentally and transmit it directly to paper without the necessity of physically having to hear it first. Ensemble works were first sketched in a piano score. Pencilled indications of the projected instrumentation were added, and, finally, a full score was extrapolated. There is no evidence in the pencil holographs (manuscripts in his own hand) seen by this writer that there was an arduous process of working out material from basic elements such as thematic germs, or any extensive revision of the first completed version of a piece. In the latter respect we seem to encounter a rather facile composer who was able to commit to paper something close to a finished product without extensive rewriting. That is not to say, however, that he wrote in haste, without preparation or sufficient gestation of musical thought.

Major revisions such as reorchestration were usually made after a considerable lapse of time and for some situation which called for modifications in the size of the ensemble as was the case with the ballets *El Fuego Nuevo*, *Caballos de Vapor*, and *La Hija de Cólquide*, or a change in performance medium—a rewriting of the choral work *Llamadas* as the orchestral *Paisajes Mexicanas*. In either case, the musical content of the matrix compositions remained intact. The enormous amount of time and effort expended on the composer's opera *The Visitors* was directed toward clarification of the vocal lines through instrumental doublings and rescoring accompaniments.

It becomes clear in talking with Chávez's daughter and his associates that he composed every day when his professional calendar would allow it. He never took vacations and he worked under a rigorous and constant self-discipline. Olga Morales, who was employed as his personal secretary in New York between 1974 and 1977, discloses the regimen Chávez followed. He would arise at 8:00 A.M., prepare his own breakfast, then compose until about 2:00 P.M. when he would break for lunch. He would also work in the evening—composing, writing, and/or studying—in preference to attending shows, concerts, or parties, or dining out. He told Ms. Morales that he was at his happiest writing music.[74]

Chávez would not allow a work to be published until he had heard it performed and had a chance to make any adjustments or corrections prompted by the performance.[75] Arthur Cohn recalls that the elaborate thirty-point checklist the composer devised for typesetting and printing preparation was the most thoroughgoing he had seen in the music publishing industry.[76] But once printed, a work was not exempt from later functional revision, as with the piano and violin concertos, for example. To encourage publishers to either publish or release materials under consideration for publication, and to represent him in matters of copyright, Chávez engaged the legal firm of Bernays and Eisner in 1967. Shortly thereafter that firm was succeeded by Freedman and Kolins. Ellis Freedman (no relation to the earlier Freedman) took over the composer's file in 1972 and at this writing still manages the legal negotiations relating to publishing and copyright for the composer's estate.

The Final Years

On January 1, 1974, Chávez leased an apartment at No. 1 Lincoln Plaza in New York. The building also houses the main offices of ASCAP (The American Society of Composers, Authors, and Publishers) of which Chávez had long been a member, and it stands opposite Lincoln Center for the Performing Arts. Chávez spent as much time here as he could after his own country had let him down in 1973. There were various honors bestowed on him in Mexico, and he carried through with his National College lecture concerts (through 1976), but the final opportunity for great service he could have rendered to the country had been dissipated by the orchestra strike.

Chávez was called upon to conduct a concert at the Ninth Interamerican Music Festival in Washington, D.C., on May 9, 1978. The concert, originally assigned to conductor José Serebrier, was given to Chávez on Serebrier's request as his own homage to the Mexican composer. Chávez, in failing health, fulfilled the engagement, premiering his *Concerto for Trombone and Orchestra* with Per Brevig as soloist. This was to be his final conducting appearance.[77]

An article in *Excelsior*, April 24, 1975, quotes Chávez as saying,

Let me complete my work as a composer in peace. I am dedicated to that. I am not able to judge the present musical situation [in Mexico]. I am seventy-five years old; I have only five or six years remaining.

The last remark would seem to indicate that Chávez suspected the seriousness of his illness, the malignancy that gradually weakened him in the final few years. Exploratory surgery performed late in 1975 by Dr. Trifón de la Sierra confirmed the presence of cancer.[78] Unfortunately his property in Mexico—the home in Las Lomas de Chapultepec in Mexico City, the house and land in Acapulco, and the house in Cuernavaca—had to be sold to pay off debts he incurred in support of his son Augustín's business ventures. Carlos and Otilia moved in with their daughter Anita in the Coyoacan suburb of Mexico City when they were no longer able to care for themselves. Otilia died April 28, 1978. The composer was revising the orchestration of his opera *The Visitors* when he died, August 2, 1978.

Who will be the next to carry the "lyre of Orpheus" in Mexico? That is yet to be answered. What is certain is that it was never more proudly borne, more firmly held, nor more eloquently played than by that nation's most important musician of this century, Carlos Chávez.

2

Solo Instrumental Works

Chávez wrote most of his solo instrumental music for the piano. There are five pieces for other unaccompanied solo instruments: *Three Pieces* (1923) and *Feuille D'Album* (1974) for guitar; *Upingos* (1957) for oboe, incidental music for Salvador Novo's production of *Hipolito* by Euripides; *Invention III* (1967) for harp, to commemorate the seventieth birthday of French composer-teacher Nadia Boulanger; and *Partita* (1973) for solo timpani.

Piano

In 1936 Chávez performed in a concert series in New York City called "Modern Masters." The series also featured Ernst Toch, Serge Prokofiev, Aaron Copland, Alexander Tansmand, and Paul Pick.[1] Earlier he had appeared in concert with the Copland-Sessions series as a pianist. As an artist on the instrument, it is not surprising that his music for the piano constitutes the largest body of works in his output: about thirty percent of the total. This music mirrors his technical mastery and his understanding of the piano's capabilities for projecting his own musical personality. It was his piano music that brought him his first publications, in Mexico City by Wagner and Levien in 1920, and in Berlin by Bote und Bock in 1923.

The piano compositions span a period of sixty years, from 1915 (he omitted some earlier works from his catalog) to 1975. He began to compose for the piano at age nine—"simple conventional pieces"—when he started his study of the instrument.[2] Later, through Luis Ogazón, and by means of his own self-study, he became acquainted with a great wealth of Classical, Romantic, and Impressionistic piano repertory. Much of his piano music shows his debt to traditional forms and principles: the sonatas, the sonatina, the waltzes, the etudes, the fugues, and the preludes. But the more novel side of his creative nature finds expression in works bearing titles like *Polygons*, *Unity*, *Blues*, *Fox*, and *Invención*.

Chávez had been fond of improvising at the keyboard since childhood. According to his own account, he would often launch into "crazy tirades" at the piano which he never intended to write down.[3] But these spontaneous exercises must have served to vent and nourish his more experimental inclinations. There are the arrangements of Mexican songs for piano, mainly miniatures lasting two to three minutes each, but also compositions of extended length like the *Sonata Fantasia* (1917), a twenty-five minute opus.

Sonatina for Piano

In 1924 he wrote three sonatinas—for piano, violin and piano, and cello and piano—which bear the mark of his preoccupation at that time with Indian nationalism. They exude the indigenous traits of driving rhythm, modal scales, persistent recurrence of melodic and rhythmic motives, linear writing, and brutish dissonance. The *Sonatina for Piano* was his first music published in the United States (in 1930). Aaron Copland, who performed the *Sonatina* at a London concert in 1931, noted that its Mexican flavor, free from any actual quotation of indigenous themes, was achieved by the composer's "rethinking the material until only its essence remained."[4]

The *Sonatina* is a one-movement piece in four sections, with the fourth section a literal repetition (though at a slower tempo) of the opening twenty-two measures. Triple divisions of the beat either alternate with or superimpose themselves over the prevailing duple beat divisions to produce a peculiarly Mexican rhythmic quality. Also contributing to the indigenous character is the ostinato passage in section three (Example 1).

Example 1.   *Sonatina for Piano*, mm. 63–66.

Tercera Sonata (Third Sonata)

Early in 1928, Chávez turned his attention away from the Mexicanism of his sonatinas toward a more international, but still highly personal style in his *Third Sonata for Piano.* He titled it simply *Sonata for Piano,* but the label *Tercera Sonata* in the published score shows its correct chronological position. The piece, dedicated to Aaron Copland, was premiered on April 22, 1928, at a Copland-Sessions Concert of Contemporary Music in New York's Edyth Totten Theatre. The composer as solo artist revealed a daring new step in the evolution of his musical style.

Chávez chose a four-movement architectural plan with contrasting movements, of which I, II, and IV bear kinship with sonata form in the return of material at adjusted pitch levels. But the first movement appears in retrospect to serve as an extended introduction to the faster and lengthier second movement. Movement three is fugal with its four-strand linear construction, alternation of expositions and episodes, and permutations of the thematic subject, all of which befit its Baroque-engendered formal procedure.

The work is charged with dissonant chromatic sonorities which strike the ear like chips of granite, but which alternate with more consonant chords and octaves in a rapid oscillation of tension and release. The rhythm measures up to the harmonic complexity in the irregular meters (like $3\frac{1}{2}/4$ and $1/12$), the frequent changes of meter, the abundant superimposed duplets, triplets, and quadruplets, and the syncopation that infuses the final movement with a tinge of 1920s jazz. A predominantly angular melody, often doled out in recurrent miniature cells, is particularly effective in the fugal third movement where placement of the fugue subject successively at different pitch strata within the same scale cements a firm modal organization of the movement. The fugue reaches its climactic point at measure 28 as the melodic subject appears simultaneously in doubled and halved note values, and as each of these variants is imitated in a dove-tailed stretto.

The four movements of the *Third Sonata* are not only individually distinctive, but are also somewhat uneven. Pianist Robert Floyd perceives the second movement as rather aimless and less compressed than the other three.[5] In general the work is tautly drawn and harshly dissonant; it presents a definite challenge to the listener, especially on first hearing. Aaron Copland has acknowledged the inaccessibility of the work to anyone less than a "Chávez adept" like himself. He believed Chávez to imply in this startling creation, "This is how it is, and you can either like it or leave it."[6]

Seven Pieces for Piano

Between 1923 and 1930 Chávez composed seven short pieces, each of two to three minutes duration, which were later published together as *Seven Pieces for*

Piano. Their brevity is compensated for in a compactness and distillation of material, especially in *Polygons* and *36*. Both feature frequent meter and tempo changes, cover the complete range of the instrument, and are replete with harmonic intervals of the seventh and ninth. Example 2 shows the motivically-built opening theme of *Polygons* (1936) which combines lyric melody with dissonant accompaniment. Reiterations and elaborations of this theme and the motives constituting it recur in a rondolike manner to bind the piece into a cohesive unit. Contrast is achieved with tempo and texture changes in the sections separating the rondo theme.

Example 2. *Polygons*, mm. 1–3.

© *Copyright 1961 by Mills Music, Inc. Used by permission of Belwin-Mills Publishing Corp.*

Unity (1930) maintains an essentially two-voice texture in which the almost constant flow of triplets is broken by unpredictable periodic insertion of duplet or dotted-eighth-sixteenth patterns (Example 3). A quiet, expressive melody comes in occasionally to relieve the overall perpetual motion effect. The repeated-note hammerstroke figure,  , adds its own "unity" by intermittent appearances in the piece.

Parallel diatonic seventh intervals infrequently invade the prevailing harmony, which itself is largely a consequence of the two meandering and colliding contrapuntal lines.

Example 3. *Unity*, mm. 6–8.

© *Copyright 1961 by Mills Music, Inc. Used by permission of Belwin-Mills Publishing Corp.*

Unity is clearly the most technically demanding piece in the set. Copland acknowledged that the *Seven Pieces* are not easily approached, but recommends starting with *Solo*, then *36*, and finally *Unity*. He praised their "personality, clarity, and sharpness of outline."[7]

Ten Preludes

The *Ten Preludes* of 1937 exhibit a departure from the Indianism of *Unity* and the chromaticism found in *Polygons* while showing a line of development from the polyphony of *Sonata III*. Pentatonic scales are avoided, and chromaticism gives way to a strict dependence on diatonic scales in the first six *Preludes* (in which only white keys are used). Their clarity and concision, enhanced by the prevailing two-voice structure, were presaged by the outer movements of *Sonata III*. The style of the *Preludes* is generally less militant than earlier works owing to the moderation of percussive effects and the focus on linear writing. *Prelude V* is the most "Mexican" due to the pervading use of the rhythmic figure 2/4 ♪♪ ♩ ♩

Chávez's original purpose was to write a piece in each of the seven diatonic modes. But, after completing the seventh *Prelude*, he proceeded to compose VIII and IX bimodally (introducing accidentals as needed), and X which is strictly a tonal piece. He intended to make them easy pieces, but as it turned out, they pose formidable demands to the performer.[8]

The background unit of note values, established at the outset of each *Prelude*, runs as a continual thread in motor-rhythm through the piece with virtually no interruption. This procedure preserves a single mood in each piece in a manner that harkens back to the Baroque theory of affections. In *Prelude VIII*, one of the two "bimodal" numbers, Chávez uses F# in alternation with, and sometimes juxtaposed (in a cross relationship) to F♮. A similar exchange between Bb and B♮ later in the piece imparts balance, on the plagal or subdominant side to the F - F# alternation. (No other accidentals appear in *Prelude VIII*.) The only suggestion of a "Mexican" rhythmic quality in the *Prelude* is the use of hemiola—substituting groupings of six background units into two triplets instead of three duplets— which occurs intermittently after its introduction in measure 6. Though meter signature changes are infrequent, Chávez is not at all faithful to the meter indicated. For example, the beginning of *Prelude VIII* has a metric pulse of 3/4 despite its *alla breve* signature (Example 4). His triumph over the "tyranny of the barline" is reminiscent of Stravinsky.

Throughout the *Preludes*, care is taken to have the two main voices share equally in the melodic presentation. Each voice is set in relief by virtue of abundant contrary motion and by frequently shifting the smaller note values from one voice to the other.

Example 4. *Prelude VIII*, mm. 1–3.

Etudes for Piano

At the invitation of UNESCO, Chávez composed, in 1949, four etudes for piano in commemoration of the centennial of Chopin's death. The single etude published as *Estudio IV* in 1949 was completed in Paris in time for the commemorative performance on October 3, 1949, by Elene Pignari at the Salle Gaveau. The other three etudes (published as *Three Etudes for Piano*) were completed afterward in Mexico City and finally premiered there in 1969 by María Teresa Rodríguez in one of the composer's lecture-concerts at the Colegio Nacional (October 4).

Chávez attempted to capture the essence of the Polish composer's music from a contemporary Mexican viewpoint without emulating him. In *Estudio IV*, he concentrated on certain specific technical problems: alternation of unisons and octaves and wide interval leaps in the left hand; rapid double-note and triple-note chords in the right hand; and the hemiola rhythmic effects inherent in 6/8 meter. At the fast tempo indicated (♩. = 126) the constant stream of eighth notes offers an imposing challenge to the performer.

Specific aspects of technique are encountered in each of the *Three Etudes for Piano*. In the first, there are rapid successions of unrelated triads, initially in the right hand, then in both hands, and finally in the left hand. Chromaticism in this study piece runs high as do passages in polychords, in which the two hands play different triads simultaneously (Example 5a). There are also passages in which two different diatonic scales come together in the upper and lower registers forming dual planes of tonality (Example 5b).

Etude II is an exercise in lyric melody at an extremely slow tempo. There is a steady increase in complexity as smaller note values and syncopation are gradually introduced and intensified. Rhythmic activity reaches its apex with both hands engaging in chromatic double-note chords in sixteenth-note values. A return to the Tranquilo opening material rounds off the etude. Expanding leaps of

Example 5.   *Etude I* from *Three Etudes for Piano.*

a. m. 73
♩ = 120

b. m.m. 47–48.

up to a twelfth in both hands vault through various eighth-note syncopations in 6/8 meter in *Etude III.* This is the most chromatic etude of the four. Rapid successions of two-note sonorities in the right hand, and then in the left, combine to form polychords at a quiet dynamic level just before the final D major chord.

Invención

Chávez wrote three compositions labelled *Inventions:* for piano (1958); for violin, viola, and cello (1965); and for solo harp (1967). The *Invención* for piano is an important milestone, for with it he committed himself to a structural principle he had probed in 1933 (*Soli I*), the idea of nonrepetition. In his fourth Charles Eliot Norton lecture at Harvard (1958), he delivered a polemic entitled "Repetition in Music" in which he examined the skillful use of repetition by, among others, Beethoven and Stravinsky. He also acknowledged the human preference for symmetry and the arguments for corroboration of material to achieve this human "need" in musical creation. While not denying the "infinite possibilities that still may lie [ahead]" for repetition, he advanced the notion that repetition and variation can be replaced by constant rebirth, "a stream that never comes back to its source . . . always linked to and continuing its original source, but always searching for new and unlimited spaces."[9]

He saw in this concept a vital alternative to the time-honored rules for reiteration, variation, and development. Chávez often stated that he disdained rules in composing, preferring to rely on his own musical instincts which were themselves directed by his total life experience. If nonrepetition is not a "rule," perhaps it should be called a "nonrule," or the antithesis of rules governing recurrence in a musical work. At least it is a procedure, and procedures can only be measured by the quality of the resulting product.

One might expect a sameness of style, texture, mood, and material to be the end result of such conscious avoidance of repetition. But this is not the case of *Invención* for piano. Elements of contrast are summoned time and again in the constant renewal of creation: each antecedent idea spawning its own consequent idea, and the latter becoming the new antecedent. *Invención*, an eighteen-minute composition, was given its official premiere by William Masselos in Cambridge, Massachusetts, on April 14. It had received an unofficial premiere by the same pianist shortly before at the Maison Français in New York.[10] One gets the feeling on hearing *Invención* that an amalgamation has taken place, one which fuses the rhythmic complexity of the *Seven Pieces*, the contrapuntal voice independence of the *Preludes*, and the extreme chromaticism of the *Etudes*, but of course, without the structural repetition occurring in those predecessors.

Sonatas V and VI

The last two piano sonatas, written in 1960 and 1961 respectively, deserve mention because they are atypical when compared to the rest of the composer's output. Written during the years Chávez directed the Composition Workshop in the National Conservatory (1960–64), they embody principles followed in that instructional program. Students wrote study pieces using specific Classical, Romantic, or Impressionistic compositions as models. In the first stage, they relied strictly on the harmonic scheme, thematic character and distribution, and formal plan of the model. This exercise completed, they then wrote an original piece in the same style.

Sonatas V and *VI* seem to conform to this two-stage procedure. *Sonata V* bears the subtitle, "according to the harmonic scheme of Mozart's *Sonata K 533/494*." It is still in manuscript and was unavailable for this study. *Sonata VI*, however, has been published (in 1965) and is commercially recorded (Genesis 1008). It is decidedly Mozartian in design and style. Functionally tonal and triadic, its outer movements are in Ab major (and in sonata and theme and variations forms respectively). The lyrical Andante middle movement is in the subdominant key of Db major.

As in *Soli II* (1961) for woodwind quintet, in which Chávez showed he was conversant with twelve-tone technique, he has demonstrated in these two sonatas (or at least in *Sonata VI*) the ability to handle a very traditional Classical idiom of expression.

Estudio a Rubinstein

Artur Rubinstein was paid homage in September, 1974, by the Israel Music Festival when it established a Piano Master Competition in his name. Chávez, one of the composers asked to contribute music in commemoration of the event, presented Rubinstein with a rapid-fire study in minor seconds entitled *Estudio a Rubinstein.*

This etudelike piece is a *perpetuum mobile* in which left- and right-hand harmonic intervals of the minor second alternate in a varying array of patterns within a continuous flow of sixteenth-note sextuplets at the rapid tempo of ♩ . = 74. The opening sextuplet configurations are shown in Example 6. Lasting just under three minutes, the piece ends in a thundering cascade of parallel minor seconds in contrary motion stretching to the outer reaches of the keyboard.

The following extract from Rubinstein's letter of appreciation to the composer speaks for itself: "I have always had great admiration for your strong and innovative work, and the composition you have dedicated to me proves it one more time."[11]

Example 6. *Estudio a Rubinstein,* beginning.

Cinco Caprichos

American pianist Alan Marks commissioned Chávez to write *Cinco Caprichos (Five Capriccios)* in 1975. Marks premiered them, together with *Estudio a Rubinstein,* at the 92nd Street YMHA in New York on March 16, 1976. The *Caprichos,* like *Invention,* are "nonrepetitive" compositions; however, there is symmetry imposed on their overall design. *Caprichos I, III,* and *V,* the faster movements, are "full of starts, hesitation, and changes of intention," while the second and fourth are slower, more sustained, and more contemplative.[12] The *Caprichos* were Chávez's final compositions for the piano, composed during a period of personal turmoil—at the time he became aware of his terminal illness. The sudden shift of ideas suggests restlessness and harsh introspection, but at the same time, the composer is in full command of his musical resources. Chávez gave Marks specific direction to play the *Caprichos* "dry" and with "brusque fortissimos."[13]

Guitar

Three Pieces for Guitar (begun in 1923) was composed at the suggestion of Andrés Segovia and Pedro Henríquez Ureña. The second and third movements were shown to the famous guitarist before the first movement was completed. Segovia was not pleased, and *Three Pieces* was left unfinished. Many years later, Jesús Silva, who had requested a guitar piece from Chávez, was shown the completed movements. He found them wholly suitable, and, with that impetus, Chávez completed the first movement (García Morillo, 28).

A primitive, indigenous quality, achieved primarily through the use of pentatonic scales, identifies the period of origination of the *Three Pieces*, a time when the composer was heavily involved with Indianism. The introductory Largo depends entirely on pitches from the five-note scale C, D, E, G, A. In the second part of the first movement (marked Poco allegro), that scale alternates with and combines with a different pentatonic scale—E, F#, G#, B, C#, as seen in Example 7. Flint-hard augmented octave harmonies help to produce the neo-primitive aura of the first movement. The second movement is a small ternary form whose outer sections, in their austerity, conjure up a dark, forboding past. Framed between the first and third sections is a more expressive melody in a higher register but still of markedly Indian visage. The third movement contains a reminder of the chains of arpeggiated chords found in the Poco allegro section of the first movement. Pentatonic melodies, and harmonies derived from them carry *Three Pieces* to a dramatic close.

Example 7.   *Three Pieces for Guitar,* mm. 15–16 (written pitch).

Probably the most performed of the solo instrumental works are the *Three Pieces for Guitar* and the piano *Preludes.* The others, it can safely be said, are little known. More exposure of this substantial segment of Chávez's production is needed in order that its merit may be better assessed and that its proper position in twentieth-century repertory be found. A step in that direction has been taken in RCA Mexico's decision to record all of the solo piano works of Chávez and to issue them in a single multi-disc album; the solo artist is the composer's protegée María Teresa Rodríguez.

3

Chamber Music

Chávez composed his first string quartet in 1921. In 1950, Herbert Weinstock described the piece as the "first to speak the composer's own voice," saying that it "promises almost everything that he has since created."[1] Since only one earlier piece of chamber music appears in his catalog (*Sextet for Piano and Strings*, 1919), it is safe to say that he did not seriously begin to write chamber works until his craft had reached a certain degree of maturity. He was secure enough with the *Sextet* to program it side by side with the works by the most renowned modern composers in his 1925–26 Concerts of New Music in Mexico City.

For his earliest chamber music Chávez used the more traditional ensembles: piano sextet (1919); string quartet (1921); sonatinas for piano, violin and piano, and cello and piano (1924). But works for standard ensembles are sprinkled through the catalog to as late as 1969, and they constitute about one-half of his chamber music output. Comprising this group are: four string quartets (1921, 1932, 1943, and 1964), the second and fourth for violin, viola, cello, and double bass; a string trio—*Invention II*, 1965; three works for violin and piano—*Sonatina* (1924), *Three Spirals* (1934), and *Variations* (1969). The only piece for woodwinds in a usual grouping is *Soli II* (1961) for woodwind quintet (flute, oboe, clarinet, horn and bassoon).

For nontraditional, or completely new ensembles Chávez wrote about ten pieces. *Energía* (1925) is for a mixed group of nine string and wind instruments. For homogeneous wind ensemble he wrote the *Sonata for Four Horns* (1929) which he later orchestrated as the *Concerto for Four Horns and Orchestra* (1937). The first *Soli* (1933) uses oboe, clarinet, trumpet, and bassoon, and *Trio* (1940) is an arrangement of music by Debussy and Falla for flute, harp, and viola. For *Xochipilli, an Imagined Aztec Music* (1940), he added to the four wind instruments—piccolo, flute, Eb clarinet, and trombone—percussion parts for six players. The success of *Xochipilli* may have helped to engender his two pieces for percussion ensemble: *Toccata* (1942) and *Tambuco* (1964). (*Partita for Solo Timpani* of 1973, though, not properly speaking a chamber work, should be cited among his music for percussion instruments.)

The music for his ballet *The Daughter of Colchis* (1943) was composed for a double quartet of winds and strings (string quartet plus flute, oboe, clarinet, and bassoon). The composer extracted No. I, and Nos. VI through IX for a suite for double quartet, and the three string movements of the suite were re-designated as *String Quartet No. 3*. Completing the list of chamber music is *Soli IV* (1966) for horn, trumpet, and trombone.

Energía for nine instruments

Edgard Varèse wrote a letter to Chávez on July 14, 1925, asking him to write *"quelque chose"* ("something") for the coming concert season of the International Composers Guild. He answered with *Energía*, a piece for nine instruments in a mixed ensemble consisting of piccolo, flute, bassoon, horn, trumpet, bass trombone, viola, cello, and double bass. Completed too late to be performed in New York as intended, the work received its premiere on June 11, 1931, at the Second Panamerican Concert in Paris, conducted by Nicolas Slonimsky, which also included music by Pedro Sanjuán, Carlos Salzedo, Alizandro Caturla, and Varèse.[2]

As its title implies, there is nothing static about *Energía*. In its three main sections played without pause, there are no blocks of chordal sound to halt the flow of the competing contrapuntal melodies. Each instrument makes its own timbral voice heard in short spurts of melody, and the instruments combine in a myriad of colors (and noises) within the thinly textured fabric. Clearly drawn passages in polytonality, as in the case cited in Example 8a, occur with moderate frequency. Starkly primitive drumlike noises are mustered from the strings playing repeated dissonant, multi-stopped chords (Example 8b). Polyrhythms

Example 8.   *Energía*
a. m. 19.   b. m. 33.

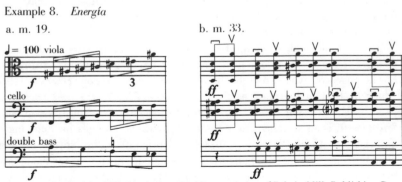

© *Copyright 1968 by Mills Music, Inc. Used by permission of Belwin-Mills Publishing Corp.*

such as two notes against three, three against four against five, and five against six, become a mannerism of the dynamic and energetic six-minute piece.

After a 1932 performance of *Energía* at a League of Composers concert in New York, Marc Blitzstein described it as "hard and athletic, [having a] galvanic charm that goes with health and with complete unconcern with nuance or suavity."[3]

Soli I for oboe, clarinet, trumpet, and bassoon

With *Soli I*, Chávez fulfilled a commission by the League of Composers for a tenth anniversary commemoration piece in 1933. Oboe, clarinet, and bassoon are joined by a trumpet to form the mixed consort of winds, and each instrument occupies the forefront for one of the four movements. The title comes from the fact that, while each instrument is featured in turn, the other instruments do not lose their soloistic independence, being only seldom relegated to an accompanying role in the essentially contrapuntal texture.

Jazzlike syncopation pervades the first movement in which the main solo instrument is the clarinet. Without pause between movements, the other three instruments take their turn: the bassoon in a sustained, expressive melody under the flare of the triple-tonguing trumpet; the oboe with a plaintive Indianesque theme in the Molto lento movement; and finally, the trumpet in the fourth movement (Vivo) alive with hemiola syncopation and duplet superimposition over triplets in 6/8 meter. The frenzied, driving rhythm in the fourth movement forecasts, to some extent, the perpetual motion effects of *Sinfonía India* (1935).

This is the first work the composer acknowledges as having been organized, to some degree, by means of nonrepetitive writing. He cites the oboe and trumpet themes, in their respective movements, as conceived with norepetition in mind.[4] Example 9a shows the trumpet melody beginning its renewing course in the fourth movement. Despite the composer's stated intention not to repeat, he does allow a very similar variant of the melody later in the movement (Example 9b).

Example 9. *Soli I*, fourth movement.
a. mm. 1–4.

b. mm. 38–40.

Three Spirals for violin and piano

The first movement of *Three Spirals* for violin and piano was published in 1935 with the title *Spiral* and was introduced by violinist Joseph Szigetti in a Town Hall recital in New York on January 30, 1937. Movements two and three were added later (they are not mentioned in García Morillo's 1960 biography). Mills Music International published the complete work in 1969.

Three Spirals is a cyclically unified chamber work which is contrapuntal in texture and chromatic in its pitch resources. The outer movements are repetitive, each having a substantial portion of its opening section reiterated later in the movement. Short germinal motives in various permutations provide the basis for the developing melodic material in these movements. The motives at the beginning of the scherzolike first movement are seen in Example 10a and b. A new motivic idea, evolved through syncopation of the second of the earlier motives makes its first of several appearances in measure 118 (Example 10c). Threeway imitation at the octave brings the counterpoint in the movement to its highest point of interest as the coda begins in measure 285.

Example 10.   *Three Spirals*, first movement.

a. mm. 1–5.

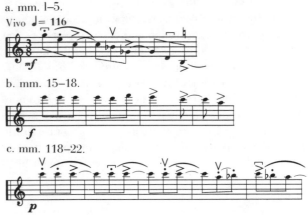

b. mm. 15–18.

c. mm. 118–22.

© *Copyright 1969 by Mills Music, Inc. Used by permission of Belwin-Mills Publishing Corp.*

The main structural element of the tranquil second movement is the melodic minor second, used to the exclusion of other melodic intervals in the violin part. Each minor second is followed by another minor second at widening, or narrowing compasses of the instrument in a seeming allusion to expanding and contracting "spirals." Chromatic scale-wise passages in the piano underscore the importance of the minor second. In the 6/8 meter of the finale, the composer once again calls forth syncopations and polyrhythms which have become idiosyncracies of his rhythmic vocabulary: superimposed 3/4 meter (hemiola) and the overlaying of binary divisions of the beat. Periodic infusion of the widening minor second "spirals" from the second movement and the repeated-note third motive from the first movement impart cyclic unification to the whole work. This conscious and careful integration of the entire piece is especially noteworthy when borne in mind that the second and third movements were later additions.

An unrelenting, angular interplay of sixteenth notes at the coda carries the work to a climactic conclusion.

Xochipilli, an Imagined Aztec Music

Xochipilli, an Imagined Aztec Music—for piccolo, flute, Eb clarinet, trombone, and six percussion players—was one of Chávez's offerings for the concerts of Mexican music presented at the Museum of Modern Art in New York in May, 1940. These concerts were given in conjunction with a special exposition called Twenty Centuries of Mexican Art. The piece is named for Xochipilli-Macuilxóchitl, Aztec god of music, dance, flowers, and love. Chávez attempted to approximate ancient Aztec music with the little concrete information there was to rely on. He used archeological percussion instruments, or modern replicas of them, like the *huéhuetl*, a hollowed-out tree trunk covered at one end by a stretched animal skin, and the *teponaztle*, a horizontal, hollow log capable of producing two different pitches. Rasps of wood or bone (*omichicahuatlis*) and rattles made of clay and copper could also be verified archeologically. The piccolo, flute, and Eb clarinet, confined mostly to pentatonic scales authenticated in surviving Aztec flutes, simulated their ancient forebears. Further documentation came from written chronicles of Aztec musical life like Fray Juan Torquemada's *Monarquía Indiana* (Seville, 1615) and from pictorial accounts such as the Aztec *Codex Florentinus*. [5]

There were no genuine Aztec melodies or rhythms to quote. Instead, Chávez sought to project the aesthetics of their music. His modern-day model was the music of the Indians of Tlaxcala which he had known since childhood, and which was deep-rooted in ancient tradition, reflecting their "sober, concise, pure, and vigorous spirit." [6]

The printed score indicates the modern percussion instruments to be used— marimba, güiro, small and medium hawks bells (copper), bongos, tenor drum, and rattles—but also contains a list of the Indian instruments used in the original performance.

The piece, lasting six minutes, is laid out in three contrasting sections. The vigorous outer portions frame a languorous Lento featuring an undulating solo in the Eb clarinet (Example 11). The "bacchic" nature of the clarinet solo intensifies with the introduction of triplets against a duple background, but the rhythmic character of *Xochipilli* as a whole is straightforward and conforms to patterns inherent in the meter (duple and quadruple patterns). Melodic and rhythmic independence of the instrumental parts is of paramount concern. The percussion instruments do join in the same rhythm in measures 223–27, but only for the sake of an insistent dramatic climax to their long soli in the third section.

Example 11. *Xochipilli*, mm. 84–91.

© *Copyright 1964 by Mills Music, Inc. Used by permission of Belwin-Mills Publishing Corp.*

The trombone (simulating a sea snail shell) sounds a haunting fanfare on an ascending fifth to conclude the composer's vivid though imaginary impressions of Aztec music.

Toccata for percussion

As previously mentioned, the *Toccata* for percussion (1942) was written at the request of John Cage for his percussion ensemble in Chicago. There was little precedent for writing exclusively for percussion, or for percussion in mixedensemble chamber music. Chávez was certainly familiar with Varèse's *Ionisation* (1933), and he most likely knew *Music for Strings, Percussion, and Celeste* (1936), and *Sonata for Two Pianos and Percussion* by Bartók. *Xochipilli* (1940) had provided him with experience in writing for a substantial aggregate of percussion. It may not be by coincidence that he wrote for the same size percussion group (six players) in the *Toccata* and *Tambuco* (1964) that he had used in *Xochipilli*.

Scored for traditional orchestral percussion instruments, the *Toccata* is in three movements with contrasting timbres: drums in the first; metal instruments and xylophone in the second; and drums and glockenspiel in the third. A roll on the side drum opens the first movement which is in a rounded repetitive form (rolls had been the nemesis of Cage's group). The composer may have been thinking of sonata form with a recapitulation at rehearsal number *19*, and coda at *28*.

Stratification and independence of the instrumental parts results in a predominantly contrapuntal texture. Imitation between bells and xylophone in the slow second movement (beginning at measure 7 of number *37*), and between timpani and bass drum (at number *47* of the third movement) is further evidence of the emphasis placed on counterpoint. Making each performer's strands of rhythmic melody heard is difficult when working with instruments of indeterminate pitch, but the situation improves in live performance when the independence can be enhanced by spatial dispersion of the ensemble.

The second movement stands out like a gem with glistening facets set between the darker shaded outer movements. For the third movement, the composer incorporates a sonatalike scheme similar to the first. The overall symmetry imparted by the formal kinship and similar instrumentation of the outer movements is readily apparent.

The fact that Cage's ensemble could not negotiate the rolls in the *Toccata* did not deter its success. The piece has remained one of Chávez's most popular and frequently performed works—probably second only to *Sinfonía India*. There have been at least eight commercial recordings made of the work up to the time of this writing.

The *Toccata* was performed as a ballet entitled *Tóxcatl* by the Academy of Mexican Dance in 1952, with choreography by Xavier Francis, and sets and costumes designed by Miguel Covarrubias. The Aztec ballet scenario is detailed in García Morillo (119–20) where the point is made that Chávez wanted the piece's original conception as pure music to be kept in mind.

Tambuco for six percussion players

Tambuco was commissioned by Clare Boothe Luce and was premiered by the Los Angeles Percussion Ensemble, William Kraft conducting, on October 11, 1965. Chávez coined the one-word title as an imitation of percussion sounds. Written almost twenty-five years after the *Toccata*, *Tambuco* still bears some resemblance to its antecedent. The two works are about the same length and both require six players. A tripartite organization is also common to both the *Toccata* and *Tambuco* although the latter is set into broad sections instead of movements.

One of the main outward differences in *Tambuco* is the much larger battery of instruments required, some of which are nontraditional—bongo drums, vibraphone, Swiss brass bells, metal rattle, and "tap-a-tap." The less conventional instruments are either diagrammed or described in the score. Liberal use of *divisi* parts increases the sound resources at times by having one or more players perform two parts on separate instruments. Another difference, due perhaps to its later origin, is the greater variety of complex rhythmic ideas found in *Tambuco*. One such case is seen in Example 12.

Example 12.   *Tambuco*, mm. 313–14.

Tambuco is deliberately nonrepetitive in design. Chávez explained that this was a "deviation from conventional contrapuntal procedures and classical developments," as well as an avoidance of any serial technique, since all of these expedients are based on repetition and symmetry.[7]

The first main section, lasting until measure 158, is full of stuttering emissions from rasps, rattles, and blocks, and güiro which remind one of "white noise" in electronic music. In the middle section, instruments of determinate pitch—glockenspiel, celesta, vibraphone, chimes, and marimba—take the forefront in an array of sonorous colors reminiscent of the *Toccata's* second movement (though much more chromatic). A brief transition by the lighter indefinite-pitched instruments with xylophone (mm. 208–15) leads to the third large section dominated by timpani, bongo and conga drums, and bass drum. A large coda begins at measure 284 with the gradual reentry of the melody instruments which gain full command of the ensemble at the fast, furious, and abrupt ending.

Solis *II* and *IV*

Chávez composed his first *Soli* in 1933. The name is indicative of the approach he used, that is, each instrument of the ensemble retains its solo quality, to a greater or lesser extent, in every movement of the work. *Soli I* was also the first composition in which he employed nonrepetition as a constructive technique. For his later *Solis*—*II* (1961), *III* (1965), and *IV* (1966)—both procedures again predominate. *Solis II* and *IV* are both written for a small wind ensemble as was the case with *Soli I*. *Soli III* is an orchestral work, but is consistent with the "soli" principle in having a concertante group consisting of bassoon, trumpet, viola, and timpani as its soloists.

Soli II appeared on the program of the Second Interamerican Music Festival in Washington, D.C., on April 4, 1961, performed by the Philadelphia Woodwind

Quintet. It was written on a commission from the Festival Committee. Terse contrapuntal melodic statements of a dry, hard, pithy, or playful nature weave in and out of the ensemble forming constantly changing kaleidoscopic colors. The composer demands execution of the most difficult figures from the instrumentalists; disjunct, fragmentary melodies in rapidly shifting registers often reach the extreme ranges of the instruments. Astringent dissonances add to the total result which is music in a convincingly personal style, not derivative of anything other than the composer's own stylistic growth.

Titles of some of the movements, such as Rondo, Aria, and Sonatina, hint at repetition of material. This suggestion is borne out in fact, but to a moderate degree, in an ironic touch counter to nonrepetitive aims. Gerard Béhague and Joan Sweeney Coombs have pointed out the twelve-tone melody, and retrograde of it, in the bassoon solo of the Aria movement.[8] There are also inversions and retrograde inversions of the twelve-tone series, and several contrapuntal combinations of them within this movement. The obviously purposeful inclusion of Viennese dodecaphonic manipulation, in such an abundant amount, is a curious inconsistency when considering Chávez's stated avoidance of this type of technique in nonrepetitive works.

An appealing work to performers and audiences alike, *Soli II* is finding a permanent place in the woodwind quintet repertory. Adding to a growing list of performances, it was played by the Charleston Symphony Woodwind Quintet at the 1980 Piccolo Spoleto Festival in Charleston, South Carolina.

Soli IV (1966) is an abstract, nonrepetitive work of ten minutes duration. The same kinds of demands are made of the instruments—in this case horn, trumpet, and trombone—as in *Soli II*, but to a higher degree. Its greater fragmentation, resulting in a pointillistic texture, requires that quick single-note shifts be made between registers of each instrument and between the instruments themselves. There are also difficult, extreme-range entrances in each part. Harsh dissonances in two- and three-note vertical sonorities often become magnified by the prominence of upper harmonics produced at fortissimo dynamic levels. A majority of the "chords" are three-note segments of the chromatic scale (Example 13).

Example 13. *Soli IV*, mm. 155–58.

Mario di Bonaventura commissioned *Soli IV* for the Hopkins Center Congregation of the Arts at Dartmouth College, Hanover, New Hampshire. It was performed there in its premiere by Robert Pierce, horn, Dominik de Gangi, trumpet, and Dean Werner, trombone, on August 9, 1967. Its performance difficulty and its uncompromising dissonance limit the possibilities for programming. Chávez advised that his nonrepetitive works require greater concentration on the part of the auditor. Without recurring motives and themes, the listener must exert extra effort to perceive the constant avalanche of new ideas. He even recommended repeated hearings, a procedure which in fact tends to dilute his basic premise as to the value of nonrepetition.

Variations for Violin and Piano

Variations for Violin and Piano was composed in response to a commission from the Lincoln Center Fund for the Chamber Music Society of Lincoln Center. It was first performed at Alice Tully Hall in Lincoln Center by Charles Treger, violin, and Richard Goode, piano, on December 12, 1969.

An angular twelve-note melody in the solo violin at the beginning suggests that a serial piece is in the offing. This proves to be the case. The opening violin statement is derived by retrograde of the first ten notes of the "theme" which is introduced by the violin in a contrapuntal duo between the two instruments at measure 3 (Example 14a). The main theme is a disjunct and chromatic pitch series of forty-two notes of which the last twenty-one notes are a retrograde of the first twenty-one.

There are seventeen successive appearances of the pitch series (or theme), then two statements of the first half only. Seams between the appearances of the series are intentionally blurred, and sections in contrasting tempos and textures do not coincide with them. The descending major seventh (Examples 14a and b) is a prominent unifying motive. In Example 14b, the major seventh comes from the retrograde of the theme, seen in its original order in Example 14a.

Example 14.   *Variations for Violin and Piano.*
a. mm. 3–5.

b. mm. 162–63.

Some of Chávez's most daring musical experiments were carried out in his chamber music: *Invention III* and *Solis I, II,* and *IV* in their nonrepetition; *Variations for Violin and Piano* in its pervading serialism; and *Toccata for Percussion* and *Tambuco* in formal coherence and unprecedented range of sonorities. Only the two percussion pieces and *Soli II* have appeared regularly on concert programs, leaving the bulk of his chamber works to be "discovered" by the musical establishment and the public.

4

Solo Vocal and
A Cappella Choral Music

Roughly twenty percent of Chávez's compositional production was in the areas of solo vocal and choral music. His twenty-five or so solo vocal works appeared between 1918 and 1967, and his choral music, numbering about fifteen pieces, was written between the years 1932 and 1975. In a few instances he employed voices as an additional "symphonic resource," specifically in the ballets *El Fuego Nuevo* (1921), *Los Cuatro Soles* (1925), and *Pirámide* (1968) which are primarily orchestral. Though a relatively small amount when compared with his instrumental output, the vocal and choral works reveal a composer adept in selecting texts suitable to his musical aims and equipped to render settings which are both compatible with and enhancing to the texts.

Chávez's taste in poetry was catholic, ranging from Medieval English to nineteenth-century European Romantic poets, and from traditional Spanish, Indian, and Mexican verses to the Mexican poets of his own day. For his first four songs (1918–1923), he drew on French verse from Victor Hugo (1802–1885), German poetry from Heinrich Heine (1797–1856), and works by the Colombian poet José Asunción Silva (1865–1896) and the Brazilian Ronald de Carvalho (1893–1935). His settings of Mexican poetry began to appear in 1923. These writers include the surrealists Carlos Pellicer (1899–1977), Ramón López Velarde (1888–1921), Xavier Villaurrutia (1903–1950), and Salvador Novo (1904–1974). Federico García Lorca (1896–1936) is the only named Spaniard represented in his vocal music.

A number of British poets attracted his muse in 1942. In that year he set poems by John Barbour (1316–1395), Nicholas Breton (1541–1626), Lord Byron (1788–1824), Percy Bysshe Shelley (1792–1822), and John Keats (1795–1821). The single American poet he selected was Archibald MacLeish (1892–

1982), former Librarian (from 1939 to 1944) of the United States Congress. Rounding out an inventory of literary sources for his vocal and choral music are traditional songs and verses from Mexico, Spain, and Portugal and Indian songs from Ecuador and Mexico.

Solo Vocal Music

In 1918, Chávez began his production of solo songs with *Extase* on a poem of Victor Hugo from the collection *Las Orientales*. This was followed in 1919 by Heinrich Heine's *Du bist wie eine Blume* and *Estrellas Fijas* by the Colombian poet Asunción Silva, and *Inútil Epigrama* from the pen of Brazilian poet-historian Ronald de Carvalho. Though these were youthful works. Chávez thought enough of them to include them in a program of his vocal music in one of his Colegio Nacional lecture-concerts in 1954. The four songs, all for voice and piano, and all in the original text language, have remained unpublished.

The next six solo songs are in two sets of three: *Tres Exágonos* [Three Hexagons], and *Otros Tres Exágonos* [Another Three Hexagons]. They were both composed in 1923 to poetry by his contemporary and friend, Carlos Pellicer. Their title comes from the fact that the poems have six lines each, similar to Japanese haikai poetry. They were labelled *Hexagons* by the poet. The first three *Hexagons* were written originally for voice and piano while the second three were provided an accompaniment of flute, oboe, bassoon, piano, and viola. After completing the second set, he arranged the accompaniment of the first three *Hexagons* for a similar ensemble, but excluding piano and having the flute and oboe double the piccolo and English horn respectively. Lines like "*hipotecando puestas del sol para edificar mi vida*" ("mortgaging sunsets to edify my life") of *Hexagon V* offer rich possibilities for color which are realized in the musical setting. The musical language in these pieces is rich in chromaticism and quartal harmony, and has a tendency toward atonality, but it is never out of keeping with tender and amatory sentiments expressed in the poetry. García Morillo has likened *Hexagons* to Schoenberg's *Pierrot Lunaire* and Stravinsky's settings of Japanese poetry in their central European musical outlook.

Todo for mezzo soprano or baritone and piano

Chávez presented a lecture at the Colegio Nacional in 1973 which he called "My Poet Friends." One of the poets addressed was Ramón López Velarde whom he had met in 1921, but whose poetry he already knew by that time. Chávez said he was bothered at first by López Velarde's use of "strange" word combinations, but grew to admire his ability to create ever new sign-symbols by his "infinite" understanding and exploitation of word meanings.

Todo (All) is in a collection of poems by López Velarde entitled *Zocobra*, published in 1919 by *Editorial México Moderno* (a publishing house founded by Carlos Chávez's cousins Augustín and Rafael Loera y Chávez). In *Todo*, the poet "speaks the subconscious without obstruction or limitation." The poem exposes elements of eroticism, mysticism, paganism, Catholicism, and existentialism which rise to the surface of consciousness and combine into new enigmatic and symbolic forms.[1]

The musical setting of *Todo* (1932) is through-composed (basically nonrepetitive) in keeping with the steady unfolding of subconscious thought in the poetry. Its several episodes, each having a notable individuality of style and texture, delineate the textual segments. The first episode is further unified by a three-note descending melodic motive which introduces several of its phrases, and which reappears in faint guises later in the song to lend unity to the whole. The pseudomodal feeling at the opening of *Todo* gradually disintegrates into an evasion of any secure tonality through the use of polytonal and starkly dissonant passages.

Three Poems for Voice and Piano

In 1938 Chávez returned to the medium of the solo song with piano accompaniment when he wrote the *Three Poems for Voice and Piano*. The poets he chose for these songs were his Mexican contemporaries Carlos Pellicer, Salvador Novo, and Xavier Villaurrutia. His first published songs, *Three Poems*, include bilingual texts in Spanish and English (English translations by Willis Wager). In the third *Poem*, Villaurrutia's "Nocturnal Rose," the composer treats the vague, surrealistic poetry with short melodic phrases of narrow compass and irregular speechlike rhythm resembling liturgical chant. The piano reinforces notes of the vocal line by paralleling, harmonizing, or sometimes distending it acoustically into higher and lower registers (Example 15).

Example 15.   *Three Poems*, "Nocturnal Rose," mm. 9–12.

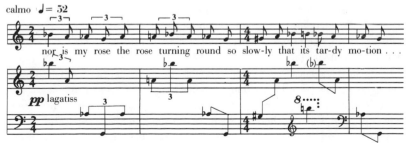

"The Reaper" (Pellicer) is in the same chantlike vocal style as "Nocturnal Rose," but is less chromatic. The accompaniment takes the form of brief episodes into quartal harmonies, parallel triads, pedal point, and contrapuntal texture. The setting of Novo's "Now from Your Eyes No Longer Shines the Starlight" is the most lyrical and impressionistic of the three. Its initial vocal phrase smacks of Debussy or Ravel. In all three *Poems* the gentle rise and fall of the melodic line corresponds to the poetic phrasing, as do the changes of texture in the episodic accompaniments. Colin McPhee's description of the composer's characteristic "incisive resonances" in these pieces[2] probably refers to a harmonic palette that is shot through with major sevenths and augmented ninths in the otherwise discreet and sedate accompaniment.

Cuatro Nocturnos [Four Nocturnes]
for soprano, contralto, and orchestra

Chávez's first solo vocal work of major dimensions was *Cuatro Nocturnos* (1939) for soprano, contralto, and orchestra. It is a fifteen-minute opus which has as its literary source four "Nocturnes" from Villaurrutia's *Nostalgia de la Muerte* [Nostalgia of Death] (Buenos Aires, 1938). Soloists appear individually in the first three movements, entitled "Nocturno," "Nocturno Sueño," [Dream Nocturne], and "Nocturno de la Estatua" [Nocturne of the Statue]. The two singers join forces in the fourth movement, "Nocturno en que nada se oye" [Nocturne in which Nothing is Heard]. Surrealistic poetry, which by its nature is an expression of the free play of the subsconscious, called for comment regarding its relationship to music by the composer. In a Colegio Nacional lecture of November, 1944, he explained that any archetypical forms or procedures in music would be incompatible with the basic tenets of surrealism. He argued that "psychic automism," for example, unforeseeable impulses, guided by the sub-conscious with all its complexity and mystery, enters into the process of musical creation and is thereby suitable for a surrealistic text.[3]

Composer-critic Virgil Thomson has suggested to this writer that Chávez never really understood how to compose for the human voice. This opinion was given in regard to the unending trials and tribulations the Mexican composer experienced with his opera *The Visitors*.[4] A hearing of *Four Nocturnes* quickly dispels this notion. Lyrical vocal melodies embody the essence of the dreamlike poetry, and the large but restrained orchestra accompanies sensitively without overshadowing the singers. The vocal lines, though challenging in respect to intonation and difficult intervals, are nonetheless "vocal" in character and idiomatic for the trained singer. Light orchestration, in a seemingly endless variety of colors, complex chromatic harmonies, polytonality, and nonpulsatile rhythm are the salient resources Chávez has assembled in surrealistic sound ambience befitting Villaurrutia's poems.

Four Nocturnes was performed by the Symphony Orchestra of Mexico in 1945 and each year of the orchestra's existence thereafter (through 1948). It has enjoyed a revival recently through performances by the National Symphony Orchestra of Mexico conducted by Chávez's former pupil Eduardo Mata, and has been recorded by the London Symphony Orchestra, with Mata conducting.

La Casada Infiel for contralto or baritone and piano

La Casada Infiel [The Faithless Wife, 1941] is a musical setting of a romantic ballad by Spanish poet Federico García Lorca. (The "Unfaithful Wife" would probably be a more accurate translation of its title although "Faithless" is how it appears in the published version.) The narrator tells of his moonlight encounter with a young "maiden" who in reality "was married already." Melodic phrases parallel the textual phrases. After the introductory line, "And so I took her to the river," Chávez carefully builds up the interest to the seduction scene with continuous running eighth notes in the accompaniment. At the conclusion of the seduction narrative, a static background of polychords, triads, and seventh chords, parcelled out in successive episodes, underscores a reflective text which begins, "That night I rode my best race . . ."

A neomadrigalian quality is achieved harmonically with a tonality that hovers around C# minor, but vacillates between Phrygian, Aeolian, and Dorian modality by periodic use of the accidentals D# and A#. A brief excursion into bitonality occurs at the line "By the avenue's last corner . . . ," where D major in the vocal line coexists with the C# minor tonality of the accompaniment (Example 16).

Lydian holds forth briefly at the beginning of the reflective text section (m. 121), but C# minor (Phrygian/Aeolian) returns at measure 137 and remains to the end of the song. The final line of text, "when I took her to the river," which is

Example 16. *La Casada Infiel*, mm. 28–30.

drawn from the opening statement, receives the same melody as its precursor, reinforcing musically the textual rounding off of the poem.

North Carolina Blues for mezzo-soprano or baritone and piano

Published together (in 1958) with *Todo* and *Dos Canciones* is the setting of *North Carolina Blues* (1942) by Villaurrutia. The poet dedicated this poem to Langston Hughes. Structurally, the poem consists of an opening refrain which recurs between oblique commentaries on the black race in the southern United States. The refrain in its complete form reads,

In North Carolina the air has a human skin feel.
Then when I caress it suddenly leaves me.
On my fingers, perspiration of one drop of water.

The composer fits the refrain to a lazy melody in D minor which contains an ambivalent A – Ab fifth scale degree (the Ab, a borrowing from the "blues scale"). The first return of the refrain is literal, both in music and text, but subsequently it is altered by key change and abbreviation, and by omission of all or part of the text. The final statement of the refrain music conveys a text other than that of the refrain, revealing a deliberately imposed musical symmetry on the nonsymmetrical poem. Each intervening episode is a separate musical and textual entity, contributing to an overall musical plan for the song of ABA-CA'DA'EA'FA' plus a coda. The first episode between refrains is accompanied by a habanera rhythm by which the composer adds, inexplicably, an Hispanic flavor to the piece.

A Cappella Choral Music

Chávez's first use of chorus was in his ballets *El Fuego Nuevo*, in 1921, and *Los Cuatro Soles*, in 1925. Works for chorus alone began to appear in 1932, at a time when the choral ensemble of the conservatory was at his immediate disposal. The choral works are in two main categories: unaccompanied, or a cappella, to be discussed here; and those scored for chorus and either orchestra or other instrumental ensemble. In the second group are the more extended works, which by nature of their concerted vocal and instrumental resources, and their lengthier texts, are more in the realm of the cantata. Discussion of the latter group is thereby relegated to Chapter 7, "Dramatic Works."

Some of the music for chorus does not fit easily into either of the two divisions mentioned. *Tierra Mojada* (1932) was initially for SATB chorus with oboe and English horn, but the published version omits the instruments. Since it is best known in its unaccompanied format, it will be treated as such in the present discussion. *Canto a la Tierra* (1946), originally for unison chorus and piano, was arranged twice by the composer: for brass septet and chorus; and second, for orchestra and chorus. None of the three versions has been published. Most of the music for chorus and orchestra also exists in versions for chorus with a piano reduction of the orchestral part. There are two compositions for speaking chorus: "Fragmento," from the ballet *Pirámide* (1968), and *Nokwik* (1975).

Texts for the a cappella choral music to 1946 come from a variety of sources: the modern Mexican poet Ramón López Velarde (*Tierra Mojada,* 1932); anonymous archaic Spanish songs (*Tree of Sorrow,* 1942); English Romanticists Keats, Shelley, and Byron (*Three Nocturnes,* 1942); medieval Scottish poet John Barbour (*A! Freedome,* 1942) and anonymous sixteenth-century verse (*A Woman is a Worthy Thing,* 1942). In the period between 1942 and 1972 he wrote nothing for a cappella chorus; however, from 1972 to 1975, six new works in this genre appeared (all six were published in 1976). *Nonantsin* (1972) is an arrangement of a traditional Nahuatl (Mexican Indian) song. In 1974 came the settings of *Epistle to be Left in the Earth* on a poem by Archibald MacLeish, and *Pastoral* and *Waning Moon* by Shelley. The composer wrote his own "text" of nonword syllables without literary meaning for *Nokwik* (1975), returning to a procedure he had used in 1968 for a ballet chorus (which has been published separately as "Fragmento" from the ballet *Pirámide*).

Tierra Mojada for SATB chorus

Tierra Mojada [Wet Earth] is one of two Ramón López Velarde poems set by the composer in 1932 (the other, *Todo* for solo voice and piano). The National Conservatory choral ensemble sang the premiere performance, conducted by Luis Sandi on September 6, 1932. Its sensual, impressionistic text begins with a portrayal of rain in a provincial town, but projects, as it develops, an awakening of the senses and an awareness of beauty, eroticism, mystery, and cynicism. A progression of contrasting word images is accommodated with frequent changes of meter and changes in the makeup of the ensemble (SATB, AB, SA, SB, and divisions into opposing pairs of voices), as well as effects such as rhythmic speech and nonword syllables. Rhythmic independence of the voices in the more contrapuntal passages is often increased by omission of some word syllables in part of the ensemble (Example 17). At the words "Evenings resembling underwater boudoirs" (no. *19*), "water" is depicted by an introductory undulating figure in the tenor in one of the more obvious uses of tone-painting.

A five-note opening melodic motive serves to unify the whole work by its intermittent returns. As is the case in its first appearance of the motive, to the words "tierra mojada," recurrences of the motive usually coincide with textual references to water, wetness, or liquid.

Example 17.   *Tierra Mojada;* number 23.

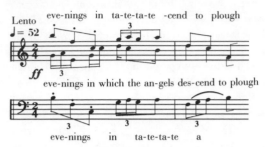

© *Copyright 1961 by Boosey & Hawkes, Ltd. Used by permission of Boosey & Hawkes, Inc.*

Tree of Sorrow for SATB chorus

Tree of Sorrow (1942) is an arrangement of an old Spanish folk song collected by Kurt Schindler (*Folk Music of Spain and Portugal,* New York, 1941). The choral setting was commissioned by Hugh Ross for a memorial concert to Schindler in Carnegie Hall on March 25, 1942. Among the other composers asked to contribute music for the occasion were Aaron Copland, Henry Cowell, Juan José Castro, Pedro Sanjuan, and Deems Taylor.[5]

This was the first choral composition Chávez conceived as an a cappella work (since *Tierra Mojada,* of 1932, had instrumental accompaniment in its original form). He treats the vocal line of the song with a rhythmic elasticity which intensifies expression from the text. The minor tonality of the folksong is preserved, but insertion of an occasional lowered second scale degree in the accompaniment superimposes a Phrygian modality which is in keeping with the melancholy of the text. Repetition of the words "Tree of Sorrow" on repeated notes in the prelude and postlude creates a frame for the main body of the piece, the folksong. *Tree of Sorrow* brings to mind Falla's settings of Spanish folksongs like *Asturiana* (which had been recommended as a model to Chávez by Paul Dukas in 1923).

Three Nocturnes for SATB chorus

Chávez's first choral settings of English verse were the *Three Nocturnes* of 1942, with poetry by Keats ("Sonnet to Sleep"), Shelley ("To the Moon"), and Byron ("So We'll Go No More A-roving"). García Morillo reports that this undertaking was intended as an exercise in preparation for an eventual opera in English (which materialized in 1953) (García Morillo, 115). The juxtaposition and mixture of homophony and polyphony give these pieces a madrigalesque quality, but their harmonic language is far from the Elizabethan practice of triads in a blend of tonality and modality. The expressive use of chromaticism has historical precedent in the late sixteenth-century madrigalists, especially Gesualdo; however, Chávez's interspersion of chords built on fourths and fifths with triads infuses these choruses with his own harmonic vocabulary. Notable tone-painting appears in "Sonnet to Sleep" where "rocking" suspensions in the music (mm. 13–18) beckon as strongly as the words do for the onset of sleep (Example 18).

Example 18.   "Sonnet to Sleep" from *Three Nocturnes*, mm. 13–18.

© Copyright 1946 by G. Schirmer, Inc. Used by permission.

A Woman is a Worthy Thing and *A! Freedome* for SATB chorus

A more conservative madrigal style was adopted for the two other choral works from 1942. *A Woman is a Worthy Thing*, on an anonymous sixteenth-century poem, and *A! Freedome*, with a text by the medieval Scottish poet John Barbour, achieve lofty suavity in their graceful diatonic melodies, triadic harmony, and reserved chromaticism. The opening section of *A Woman is a Worthy Thing* begins in imitative counterpoint which soon dissolves into luxuriant homophony. This is followed by two strophes, both beginning with the words "A woman is a worthy . . . ," which have the same music except for their final cadences. Dancelike rhythm briefly intrudes on the lyricism of the strophes. The sixteenth-century view of womanhood conveyed in the text takes on a humorously condescending tone today.

A! *Freedome*'s text is in middle Scottish which appears in the choral setting along with Willis Wager's English translation. Exalted patriotism reaches a dramatic height in the center section where the text deals with "freedom lost." A passage in sonorous parallel sixths, leading to a recapitulation of the beginning strophe, may be an intentional nod to medieval English discant style.

The late "madrigals"

Chávez returned to the medium of a cappella chorus in the 1970s with the series of six works from 1972 to 1975 (all of which were published by Tetra Music Corporation in 1976). *Nonantsin* (1972) is a supposedly traditional Nahuatl Indian song whose historical authenticity cannot be determined. Its rhymed poem concerns a young warrior who, expecting to die in a holy war, instructs his mother to explain her cries of mourning as caused by the fact that the "firewood is green." Pentatonic melodic phrases are set in a static chordal-textured sections in which the harmony is derived from the diatonic scales of C major or A major. The exotic articulations of Nahuatl poetry (facilitated by a phonetic pronunciation guide in the score) and the dark harmonic coloring of pentatonic melody admirably suit the remote and somber quality of the text.

Four "madrigals" written in 1974 are akin to the *Three Nocturnes* of 1942 in their extensive chromaticism, but they are set in a more severely angular melodic vein. The disjunct ejaculations of melody in MacLeish's *Epistle to Be Left in the Earth* are made even more intricate by their rhythmic complexity. *A Pastoral*, on an Elizabethan text by Nicholas Breton, is a lively rhythmic depiction of a shepherd wooing a maiden. She resists at first, but finally relents "in the merry month of May." This piece is a modern counterpart of the Elizabethan *ballett*, or "fa-la" madrigal, but without the fa-la-la refrain. Distribution of text syllables among the voices, often seen in Chávez's choral music, is carried to an extreme in *Waning Moon* to achieve the filigree texture suggested by Shelley's nocturnal poem (Example 19).

It is not surprising that Chávez paid such rapt attention to the joining of music and words. He had a consuming interest in poetry. The literary periodical *Gladios*, which he founded in 1915, has been mentioned. Since the 1920s, his circle of friends in Mexico City included the country's leading writers and poets. Among these were López Velarde, Pellicer, and Nova whom he referred to in a 1973 lecture as "My Poet Friends."[6]

Example 19.   *The Waning Moon*, mm. 1–3.

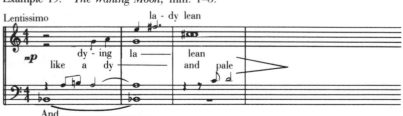

5

Symphonies and Concertos

The first large-scale composition attempted by Chávez in his apprentice years was a symphony, begun in 1915 and completed in 1918. The fact that it was never performed did not diminish his interest in writing for orchestra. Well before he began directing the Symphony Orchestra of Mexico in 1928, he showed his affinity for this medium of expression with the ballets *El Fuego Nuevo* (1921), *Los Cuatro Soles* (1925), and *Caballos de Vapor* (1926). Once he became musical director of the Mexican orchestra, performances of his music were assured. He was able to experiment, hear the results, and make adjustments as he saw fit. It was through his orchestral music that Chávez achieved his international reputation as a composer, and this body of music constitutes a large share of his most revered creative output.

The orchestral works can be classified into four categories: the six symphonies; the four concertos; arrangements of other composers' (or his own) music; and the progressive orchestral works from 1964 to 1971.[1] The six symphonies are the most traditional of the original orchestral compositions due to their reliance on repetitive forms and their greater lyricism. The works from 1964 (*Resonancias*) through 1971 (*Initium*) are the most experimental as a group, in regard to both content and form. Concerto composition extended from 1937 (*Concerto for Four Horns*) to 1976 (*Concerto for Trombone*, the last major work he wrote). The early concertos exhibit conservative features of form and material, while the *Concerto for Trombone* is more akin to the late orchestral works just mentioned. Such classification tends to convey that there is a great similarity within any one group. With Chávez each new work poses new demands, for which he sets new parameters, blazes new paths, and this results in compositions which are total, complete, and individual entities. Each is highly original in its own right while bearing the unmistakable mark of its creator.

Arrangements of music by other composers or of his own music make up the remainder of the independent orchestral music. These works include the

Chaconne in E minor by *Buxtehude* (1937) and a modern orchestration of Vivaldi's *Concerto in G Minor*, op. 6, No. 1 (1943). Nationalistic or patriotic music arranged for orchestra includes the two revolutionary songs "Club Verde" by Rodolfo Campodónico, the traditional "Adelita," and Genaro Codina's march "Zacatecas," all combined under the title *Chapultepec* (1935), and the *National Hymn* (1941) by Jaime Nunó. Also nationalistic but not truly orchestral music is his *Cantos de Mexico* (1933) for Mexican orchestra. This ensemble, consisting of a variety of ancient and modern indigenous instruments, was created for the students of the National Conservatory to provide a vehicle for the performance of music created in Chávez's composition class.

Chávez's orchestral arrangement of the *Suite for Double Quartet* from the ballet *La Hija de Cólquide* (1943) became the second of two concert suites of ballet music, the first being *Horsepower Suite* (1926). Discussion of this music appears in Chapter 7, "Dramatic Music."

All told the orchestral music is impressive in its quantity—more than twenty separate works with a total duration of about six hours. The largest share of that six hours is constituted by the six symphonies and four concertos, to be addressed presently.

Symphonies

The symphonies, excluding the 1915–18 student work cited above, began to appear in 1933 with *Sinfonía de Antígona*. This symphony grew out of incidental music the composer had written in 1932 for a Mexico City production of the Sophocles play. *Sinfonía India* (1935) is the only nationalistic work among the symphonies. It has authentic Indian themes as well as rhythms and scales drawn from what has remained of ancient Indian music in Mexico. The last four symphonies, written between 1951 and 1961, are absolute music with ingeniously planned and executed formal designs. The symphonies as a group are the most conservative of the independent orchestral works: the fourth (1953) is subtitled *Sinfonía Romántica*, and *Symphony No. 5* (1953) tends toward neo-Classicism; *Symphony No. 6* shows what a masterful constructivist the composer was in his treatment of the passacaglia finale.

Sinfonía de Antígona

In 1932 Chávez wrote seven minutes of incidental music for a Mexican production of Sophocles' *Antigone*, in the Jean Cocteau version, which was performed in the *Teatro Orientación* of the Secretariat of Public Education. Reorchestrated and lengthened to eleven minutes duration, the music became the composer's first numbered symphony, *Sinfonía de Antígona*, and was premiered on December 15, 1933, by the Symphony Orchestra of Mexico.

Imagery of Greek antiquity, evoked by means of polyphonic modal melodies, chords built on fourths and fifths, and dark wind instrumental colors, brings to mind the austere neo-Classicism of Stravinsky's *Oedipus Rex* (1927). While the one-movement symphony captures the bleak and tense spirit of the tragedy, there are no programmatic references to specific dramatic events.

Harmonically, the symphony is organized around an E tonal center which shifts between Phrygian and Aeolian modality (or Dorian and Hypodorian in the Greek system) by means of the alternation of the notes F and F#, the second scale degrees of the respective modes with their finals on E. The B Phrygian tonality which sets in at *15*, and the A Phrygian key feeling at *29* aid in polarizing the central E minor key feeling. Jesús Bal y Gay has pointed out that the notes belonging to these key centers and modes can all be derived from four disjunct tetrachords of the same genus (ABbCD, EFGA, BCDE, F#GAD).[2] Whether Chávez used this pseudo-Greek method to arrive at his tonal organization remains conjectural.

Motives grow out of germinal ideas like the chromatic three-note element played at the beginning by the bassoons (Example 20a). It is expanded by harp I at number *2* (Example 20b), by the horns at *5* (Example 20c), and in the clarinets, trumpet, and piccolo at *8* (Example 20d). Sonata form is suggested when the theme in 5/8 meter, first encountered at number *6*, returns at *27*.

Example 20. *Sinfonía de Antígona.*

a. beginning.   b. no. *2*.

c. no. *5*   d. no. *8*.

Unusual unison and octave doublings, like piccolo, clarinet, and trumpet; piccolo and Heckelphone; and oboe, clarinet, and Heckelphone, add a remote strangeness, and expressionistic outlining to the generally sparse orchestration. Multivoice, linear counterpoint in eighth notes (in 6/8 meter) lead to the double climax of the work at *24* and two measures before *27*. This pandiatonic counterpoint generates a kind of rampant motor rhythm which foreshadows some passages in *Sinfonía Índia*.

Sinfonía Índia

When the name Carlos Chávez is mentioned, the most likely word-association response will be "Sinfonía Índia." Like Beethoven's *Fifth Symphony* and Ravel's *Bolero*, *Sinfonía Índia* has become the main source of its composer's identity with the public. The immense popularity of this work has resulted in frequent programming, and in at least seven commercial recordings to date.

The symphony was written in New York in 1935 for a concert to be conducted by the composer on the CBS radio network. The conducting appearance came about at the invitation of William S. Paley, president of CBS. It took place January 23, 1936, and with it came the American debut of a major conductor and the premiere of his most celebrated work.

Like *Sinfonía de Antígona*, *Sinfonía Índia* is a one-movement composition of eleven minutes duration. The orchestra is slightly smaller, and some of the darker instrumental colors—Heckelphone, trombone III, and tuba—of the earlier work are absent. But it calls for a large battery of indigenous percussion instruments requiring four players. A list of these instruments and their modern counterparts appears in the printed score along with the composer's recommendation that the original instruments be used if available. These include *tenabari* (a string of butterfly cocoons), *grijutian* (a string of deer hoofs), water gourd, rattles, rasps, *teponaztles* (pitched drums), and *tlapanhuéhuetl* (large cylindrical drum). Indian elements derive also from the main thematic material: actual melodies of the Cora, Yaqui, Sonora, and Seri Indians collected in Mexico.

The architectural design of the work closely resembles sonata form, but there is no central development section. The introduction is rhythmically charged with constant eighth notes in frequently changing meters of 5/8, 3/8, and 2/4 in the strings and winds. A triumphant call in the trumpet completes the pentatonic melody begun by the horn over the busy rhythmic background. A brief transition, introducing light percussion, leads to the principal theme section at *9*. Here a vigorous, jerky theme from the Cora Indians rekindles the rhythmic vitality (Example 21). Development of material in this symphony takes the form of thematic repetition with varied texture and orchestration in the accompaniment, or as seen in the transition beginning at *14*, the simple melodic motive undergoes

Example 21. *Sinfonía índia, no. 9.*

subtle transformation in the frequently shifting meter (Example 22). As in the introduction, melodies from pentatonic scales in the transition (*14* to *27*) lend an Indianesque caste to material which is not authentically Indian. Free diatonic harmonies (which give the impression of being randomly selected) further reinforce the neoprimitive quality.

Example 22. *Sinfonía índia, no. 14.*

A key feeling of Bb major is maintained from the beginning until the arrival of the subordinate theme section which shifts to Eb major (no. *27*). A cantabile melody of the Yaqui Indians supplies the thematic substance for this slower section. The Eb clarinet theme is accompanied only by a water gourd (or tenor drum) and by a fragile arpeggiation in the Bb clarinet (Example 23). A gradual crescendo in texture and dynamic level in the melodic repetitions mounts to a fortissimo in the winds and strings at *42*. Here the solo horn intrudes on the Eb tonality, preannouncing the plaintive A minor Sonora Indian theme of the approaching section before the subordinate section has run its full course. The central section of the symphony, from *43* to *59*, stands in the position where a development section is normally situated in sonata form. Piccolo and horn double the melody at the outset (Example 24), and again, as in the previous sections, the sound mass increases as new material unfolds.

Example 23. *Sinfonía Índia, no. 27.*

Example 24. *Sinfonía Índia, no. 43.*

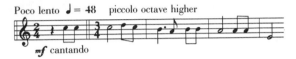

The recapitulation is normal in terms of the order of the principal and subordinate theme sections and in the change of key in the latter from Eb major in the exposition to Bb major in the recapitulation. The coda of the sonata form takes its melodic and rhythmic material from the introduction, and, on first hearing would suggest that the piece has come full circle and is about to end. However, the composer appends a frenetic finale in F major, based on a Seri Indian tune (no. 88), as a capstone to the entire work. In the finale, the strings play nothing but repeated, percussive chords in rapid triplets against occasional duplets in the melody, and finally against constant duplets from the full percussion section. This ending is remarkable for its savage energy, achieved in the rhythmic tension, the doggedly persistent repetition, and the uninhibited glissandos in the melody.

In early program notes for this symphony, Chávez explained his leanings toward the indigenous music of Mexico as follows: "I wrote this and other Indian symphonies (*Los Cuatro Soles* and *El Fuego Nuevo*) because it is the first music I heard in my life and that which has done the most to nourish my musical taste and consciousness" (García Morillo, 89).

A band arrangement of *Sinfonía Índia* by Frank Ericson was published in 1971 by G. Schirmer, Inc. (who owns the copyright of the symphony). Chávez did not authorize the arrangement, but he used it in performances with his own revisions to Ericson's instrumentation.[3]

Sinfonía No. 3

It was eighteen years before another symphony appeared. *Sinfonía No. 3* was commissioned in 1950 by Clare Boothe Luce, and dedicated to the memory of her daughter Ann Clare Brokaw. Work on it was interrupted by illness[4] and by the need to fulfill commissions for the next two symphonies. The third symphony was finally completed on January 24, 1954. The initial performance took place at the First Festival of Latinamerican Music in Caracas, Venezuela, on December 11, 1954. It earned the *Premio Caro de Boesi* for the composer, who conducted the premiere performance. Other significant performances followed: Baden-Baden, January 17, 1955, for the Festival for the Society of Contemporary Music; New York, January 26, 1956 (and days following), with the New York Philharmonic conducted by the composer; and August 27, 1956, when he led the National Symphony Orchestra of Argentina in still another playing of the new work (García Morillo, 152–53).

Unlike *Sinfonía de Antígona*, whose raison d'etre was to support a dramatic presentation, and *Sinfonía India*, which is nationalistic in its character and resources, *Sinfonía No. 3* is absolute, abstract music without any extramusical considerations beyond the *raison d'être* of its commission. The twenty-six minute symphony is laid out in four movements—Introduzione, Allegro, Scherzo, and Finale—of which the outer two are in slow tempos. The work is cyclic inasmuch as thematic material from the first movement recurs in the Finale.

A three-note descending idea, announced by the Eb clarinet one measure after *1*, becomes the chief motivic cell of the first movement. A new three-note cell appears in the first violins at *3*, and then the two are extended and joined by the oboe at *4* (Example 25).

Example 25. *Sinfonía No. 3*, first movement.

a. no. *1*.

b. no. *3*.

c. no. *4*.

The first section builds steadily to a climax at *12* where a fortissimo orchestral tutti presents a grand statement of the beginning motive. The principal motive of the second section (beginning at *14*), is a jagged, atonal melodic fragment in sixteenth-note sextuplets in a variety of configurations which had been tentatively introduced in the third measure of the symphony (Example 26a). A short bridge leads to an abbreviated recapitulation of the first two sections at *21*. The jocular "child's chant" motive at *16*, which sounds incongruous with the serious tone of the movement, becomes another important unifying element to the whole work by its return in the Finale (Example 26b).

The coda ending the first movement presents repeated octave leaps in the piccolo that forecast the octave intervals in the opening and central motive of the second movement.

Example 26. *Sinfonía No. 3*, first movement.

a. m. *3*.   b. no. *16*.

The second movement is more like the typical opening movement of a symphony by reason of its fast tempo and its sonata architectural design. It begins in D major/minor, but chromaticism gradually erodes the tonality, and a completely atonal feeling has set in by no. *36* where a tutti pyramid chord incorporates all of the tones of the chromatic scale except E. The impetuous triplet rhythm lasts through the principal theme section in brilliant orchestration leading to the concertante subordinate theme section at *50*. Here the key of A major is abandoned in favor of Eb major, a juxtaposition affording maximum tonal contrast. Further contrast at the subordinate theme section comes about with a slower tempo and changes of meter (4/4 alternating with 1/8, then 7/16) (Example 27).

The more fully scored recapitulation, at *78*, finds the subordinate theme transposed to D major (from Eb major in the exposition). The coda begins at *92* with a simultaneous treatment of the principal and subordinate themes. Strings bring the movement to a close after eight minutes of driving energy has been spent. The second movement stands out as the main focus of interest in the symphony by virtue of its greater length and solid formal structure.

Example 27. *Sinfonía No. 3*, second movement. no. *50*.

The third movement, Scherzo, opens as a fugue with five successive statements of its syncopated subject in the winds. This lithe fugue subject (which one writer called "grotesque") is shown in Example 28. An episode, made up of fragments of the subject in stretto, from *110* to *114,* is followed by a strict statement of the subject in canon at the octave which ends the section. The slightly faster second section builds gradually from a sparsely textured woodwind concertante to a dissonant full orchestral tutti, then returns again to the lighter texture. A three-measure bridge connects to the return of the fugue subject and its countersubjects in a three-statement exposition to end the movement.

After a slow, static introduction by the lower strings, harp, and English horn, two successive woodwind trios—oboe, English horn, bassoon, and Eb, Bb, and bass clarinets—play tunefully expressive passages which comprise the first formal section of the Finale. But the rather somber mood they establish is replaced by a tenacious exchange, among the entire orchestra, of groups of four sixteenth notes harmonized in minor seconds at *52.* (Chávez returned to a similar treatment of minor-second harmonies with his *Estudio a Rubinstein* in 1974). References to motives from the first movement begin one measure before *153* (the jocular, childlike motive) and at two measures before *155* (the three-note descending motive). These two motives, as well as the disjunct sextuplet melodic idea from

Example 28. *Sinfonía No. 3*, Scherzo, beginning.

the second section of the first movement, all appear in the Finale's third section beginning at *157*. A descending bass line leads to D, the opening key of the symphony, in a closing tutti chord spelled D, F#, F, G, A, C. *Sinfonía No. 3* is an intricate work in which rhythmic complexity, extended solos and solis, and daring melodic flights make it a difficult piece to perform. These factors, combined with its dissonant harmonic palette, make it less than easily accessible to the listener, at least on first hearing. But, for its originality of material, ingenuity of construction, and range of orchestral colors, it is admired by many as one of the composer's major works of art. Aaron Copland expressed the following opinion of the symphony after hearing its premiere in Caracas.

Sinfonía No. 3 . . . is very personal and uncompromising. Its four brief and connected movements have an almost sadistic force that compels attention. The symphony is powerful but not music that can be easily loved.[5]

A negative appraisal came from Franz Reinzenstein after the 1955 European premiere of the work in Baden-Baden. He attacked the symphony for its lack of structural solidity (especially in the first and fourth movements) and for being too derivative of Stravinsky's *Piano Sonata* (he refers here to the first movement of the *Sonata* and the theme from the second section of the *Sinfonía's* first movement).[6]

Symphony No. 4, Sinfonía Romántica

Symphony No. 4, which was completed in January of 1953, was premiered the following February by the Louisville Symphony Orchestra. The commission from that orchestra included an invitation to the composer to conduct the premiere. Dissatisfied with the third movement in its relationship to the symphony as a whole, Chávez detached it, and renamed it *Baile Cuadro Sinfónico*. He wrote a new Finale and added the subtitle *Sinfonía Romántica* for the published version of the symphony.

A mood of lighthearted optimism and buoyancy in the work is achieved with lyrical themes, tonal clarity, and vibrant rhythm. Cyclic construction of its three movements is more thoroughgoing than in *Sinfonía No. 3*. The two melodic ideas that supply the main thematic material in the first movement also appear prominently in the second movement (the first theme), and in the third movement (both themes). The first of the two themes has as its main feature successive downward and upward seventh leaps (Example 29a), while the second, a slower, more languorous melody, is easily identified by its initial downward minor third and major sixth (Example 29b).

The sonata-form exposition of the first movement, Allegro, begins without an introduction and is a statement of the principal theme in A major by the English

Example 29. *Symphony No. 4*, first movement.

a. beginning.

b. no. *3*.

horn (Example 29a). A light orchestral texture is produced by secondary motivic elements darting in and out of the contrapuntal accompaniment. Among these are groups of four scalewise sixteenth notes (two measures before *2*) and the repeated jazz rhythmic pattern—   ♪ ♩ ♩ ♩.   —in the horns and trumpet (one measure after *2*). Three-note ascending or descending scalewise melodic elements provide accompaniment for the subordinate theme which begins at *3*, and they assert their own melodic importance when both are present as the subordinate theme bows out at *8*. Another salient background motive consists of arching eighth notes, seen first in the exposition at three measures after *8*; this figure becomes the main feature of the retransition to the recapitulation at *19*. Contrast in the development section takes the form of a new dancelike Meno mosso, at *17*, where the rhythmic pattern   ♩ ♪♪   alternates in seesaw fashion between the double basses and timpani on the one side and bassoons and horn on the other. Musical events in the recapitulation unfold in the same order as in the exposition but with different orchestral colors. The subordinate theme, however, is transposed up a major second to the tonic key of A in the recapitulation (from G in the exposition). A terminal development section and coda follow at *32* toward a rousing fortissimo finish, ending the movement on a two-note A–D chord.

The principal theme (of the first movement), played by the first violins, introduces the Molto lento second movement. Its new countersubject, in the cellos, plants the seed—an upward major seventh melodic interval—which grows into the chief motive element of the movement (Example 30). This new thematic idea is a "head motive" whose first four notes remain essentially unchanged, but whose continuations vary, in subsequent appearances. A striking orchestration feature of the second movement is the absence of woodwinds. Chávez described this movement as "an aria entrusted to the violins and violas"

Example 30. *Symphony No. 4*, second movement.

a. beginning.

Molto lento ♩ = 42
violins I, sul G

b. four measures after no. 42.

(García Morillo, 159). These instruments play the last two-thirds of the movement in unison, while brass and lower strings furnish contrapuntal support and color variation to the aria.

The Finale, a lively Vivo movement, quotes generously from the two main themes of the first movement. But the preeminent thematic idea of the movement is a freewheeling march which first appears three measures after *54* (Example 31). The theme, in A major, is given an F major accompaniment. When the march theme returns at *79* and *100*, each time after developmental episodes, the propulsive motor rhythm, intensified by the addition of percussion, takes on a jubilant ambience. The march finally dissolves into contrary motion scales which pandiatonically set up an A major key feeling in a torrent of sixteenth notes played by the full orchestra (*103*). The piece comes to rest on a tonic A major ninth chord.

Example 31. *Symphony No. 4*, third movement. three measures after *54*.

Since the third and fourth symphonies were written close to the same time, perhaps it is not unusual to find some similarities despite their vast differences. For example, harmonization of the march theme of *Symphony No. 4* (Example 31) shows kinship in style with the subordinate theme of the second movement of *Sinfonía No. 3* (no. *50*). Also, the last three notes of the jocular, mocking motive in the third symphony (See Example 26) can be distinguished in the Finale of *Symphony No. 4* at *85* where it is appended three times to one of the treatments of the second main theme.

The original third movement of *Symphony No. 4* (still unpublished), which became *Baile Cuadro Sinfonico*, is reported by García Morillo as having a "Mexican character." He quotes a passage which shows the alternating 6/8–3/4 rhythmic nature of the *huapango* (García Morillo, 163). Perhaps this ethnic flavor was what the composer had in mind when he made the judgment that a new Finale was needed.

Sinfonía No. 5

The fifth symphony was written on a commission from the Serge Koussevitsky Foundation. This three-movement work for string orchestra was completed in Acapulco on October 4, 1953 (both *Sinfonía No. 5* and *Symphony No. 4* were thus finished before the completion of *Sinfonía No. 3*). Its premiere performance, by the Los Angeles Chamber Orchestra, took place on December 1, 1953, with the composer conducting.

Unlike the third and fourth symphonies, which are cyclic by reason of thematic relationships between movements, *Sinfonía No. 5* has three virtually independent movements. Five-part string writing is the rule; in other words, the double basses do not reinforce the cellos at the lower octave. The richness of its linear polyphonic texture can be seen in Example 32. The same example reveals an E

Example 32. *Sinfonía No. 5*, beginning.

© *Copyright 1964 by Mills Music, Inc. Used by permission of Belwin-Mills Publishing Corp.*

minor tonality at the opening of the symphony and hemiola rhythmic shifts in the second violins, violas, and cellos (mm. 2–3). The first three notes of this theme serve as a germinal melodic cell for the entire first movement. A recapitulation of the main theme, though altered, reveals that a sonata form has taken shape, but a sonata form adjusted to the composer's own needs. The needs in this case include the introduction of new thematic material in the development section (nos. *11–17*).

The second movement, beginning on the same chord that ended the first movement, is fashioned into a series of contrasting episodes in which instrumental recitative and dialogue appear to be the main goals. Expression is heightened in some of these passages by having all of the strings in unison (without octave doublings), for example, placing the violins and double basses in their extreme low and high registers respectively. The last section of this movement, lasting well over four minutes, contains one of the most eloquent extended passages of harmonics in the string repertoire. As the harmonics arrive, they repeat, in an eerie negative image, a pentatonic motive just introduced. The glassy sounds produced by harmonics (Chávez uses all of the first six harmonics) in the entire string section also give the effect of another orchestral section, sounding like distant woodwinds or bells. Fluctuating pentatonic melodies are divided pointillistically between the sections. The alternating single melodic notes, bring to mind the type of melodic style rendered by Swiss bell choirs. A muted A major triad brings this movement to an end.

A parade of six interrelated motives, first in forward order, then reversed, constitutes the thematic substance of the exposition in the Finale. The first, second, fourth, and fifth of these are shown in Example 33. A short central section, which develops the six motives proceeds to a recapitulation of the motives in forward order, and a coda. The coda, in a ruthless onslaught of thirty-second

Example 33. *Sinfonía No. 5*, Finale.

© *Copyright 1964 by Mills Music, Inc. Used by permission of Belwin-Mills Publishing Corp.*

notes, is one of those instances described by Copland in which the "sheer welter of notes thrown at the listener is almost overwhelming."

Sinfonía No. 5 is sometimes labelled a neo-Classic work due to its conventionally formed outer movements, and, perhaps, because of the controlled emotion. There is, nonetheless, sufficient subjectivity and dramatic expression, especially in the second movement, to require caution in applying the term neo-Classic.

The symphony soon became known in New York and Rome via performances there in 1954. It was reviewed favorably in these performances by, among others, Michael Steinberg, Howard Taubman, and Virgil Thomson.[8]

VI Symphony

Written for the opening of Philharmonic Hall at Lincoln Center for the Performing Arts in New York, the sixth symphony was premiered there on May 7, 1964 (a year and one-half after the opening) by the New York Philharmonic, conducted by Leonard Bernstein. The piece was dedicated to that orchestra and its conductor.[9]

This symphony is a monument to the classicism of the composer—his ability to organize vast amounts of material along classical lines. The main key feeling of the work is C, but, as is usual with his treatment of tonality, the key feeling is never maintained long without some indecisiveness of key through polytonality, or atonality.

The first movement is in sonata form, opening with the syncopated principal theme in the violins and violas shown in Example 34. A lyrical subordinate theme derived from an elaboration of the principal theme rhythm follows at measure 51, and gradually merges into the development section. A recapitulation at measure 176 restates the exposition themes in their initial order of appearance, and with the standard modulation of the subordinate theme a fourth higher. The composer resumes the development of material after the exposition, and here we

Example 34. *VI Symphony.* beginning.

Allegro energico ♩= 116
violins and violas

f cellos and bassoons

horns

double basses

© *Copyright 1965 by Mills Music, Inc. Used by permission of Belwin-Mills Publishing Corp.*

see new permutations of the principal theme such as a half-step higher (m. 308),
and inverted and in imitation (m. 313). A gradual ritardando and diminuendo in
the strings brings the scherzando coda to rest on the cellos' low C.

The second movement, Adagio molto cantabile, begins in a very thin contrapuntal texture with its melody unfolding in relay among wind instruments
starting with the trumpets. Concertante winds have been deployed with some
frequency in other symphonic works by Chávez; their use here helps to underscore the classical tone of the *Symphony VI*. Notable in this regard is the soli for
four horns at measure 358. A fortissimo G minor chord (fifth omitted) ends the
second movement and sets the stage for the grandiose passacaglia of the Finale.

The passacaglia theme of the Finale is introduced by the solo tuba to open the
movement. The theme mixes chromatic with diatonic melodic progression.
Starting on C, it makes its way back to the beginning pitch with a concluding
melodic cadence (Example 35).

Example 35.   *VI Symphony*, Finale, beginning.

In its forty-four appearances, this melody is subjected to, at times, inversion,
expansion and contraction, transposition, and migration into the middle and
upper voices. It is even given a fugal treatment starting at measure 708. As a
fugue subject, it takes on the countersubject and bass line seen in Example 36. C
major tonality is secured one final time at the conclusion with a gigantic C major
chord in the full orchestra. Thus ends one of the composer's most masterful
symphonic movements.

In joining historical polyphonic and homophonic processes with pantonality
and atonalism, Chávez has achieved "the marvellous task of taking the past and
returning it as part of the future."[10] Irving Kolodin, in referring to this work, said
of its composer:

> The facility with which Chávez manipulates his materials shows the practical hand of one.
> who at sixty-five years of age. builds with sonorities as others are able to build with stone.
> Certainly in the 43 [sic] variations of the passacaglia Finale. Chávez has raised a cathedral
> of sonorities to his faith. which is clearly music.[11]

Example 36. *VI Symphony*, Finale. mm. 742–45.

Concertos

Chávez's four works labelled concertos are the *Concerto for Four Horns and Orchestra* (1937), the *Concerto for Piano with Orchestra* (1938), the *Concerto for Violin and Orchestra* (1948), and the *Concerto for Trombone and Orchestra* (1976). A cello concerto, begun in 1975, was projected as a four-movement work but was not completed (Chávez finished 153 measures of the first movement and a theme for the second movement). Another concertolike work for soloists (bassoon, trumpet, viola, and timpani) and orchestra—*Soli III*—appeared in 1967. A further concerto undertaking was the reorchestration of Vivaldi's *Concerto Grosso*, Op. 6, No. 1, made in 1943. The "concertante" principle of a group of soloists within the orchestra is not limited to the *Concerto for Four Horns* and *Soli III*; the symphonies display innumerable passages for combinations of solo instruments in concertante style. Much of the uniqueness of the composer's orchestral style is attributable to his imaginative mixtures of solo orchestral colors, and his adroit handling of solo groups.

Concerto for Four Horns and Orchestra

The Sonata for Four Horns, written in 1929, became the basis for the *Concerto for Horns*. The *Sonata* was first performed at a National Conservatory concert in Mexico City in 1931. In 1937, Chávez orchestrated the first two movements of the *Sonata* for an orchestra consisting of Eb clarinet, two Bb clarinets, bass clarinet, English horn, three bassoons, timpani, and strings in addition to the four solo horns. The preface to the printed score states that the *Concerto* remains exactly the same in musical content as the *Sonata* "except for the changes in instrumentation implied by the concerto treatment." In its two-movement form, the piece was played at the Eighth Festival of Chamber Music in Washington, D.C., on April 11, 1937, with Chávez conducting the Coolidge Festival Orchestra. Orchestration of the third movement was added in 1938, and the piece was first performed in its entirety in the 1939 season of the Symphony Orchestra of Mexico with the composer conducting. In 1966, Chávez reorchestrated the *Concerto* and destroyed the original orchestration. The published score (1967) preserves this final orchestration.

The omission of flutes, oboes, and trumpets bestows an overall dark shading on the orchestra. The two homogeneous quartets of woodwinds—one having four clarinets and the other comprised of English horn and three bassoons—foreshadows the restrained color range (quartets of woodwinds and strings) of *La Hija de Cólquide* (1943). The four horns are most often used concertedly, but the melodic importance and technical demands in each part require four virtuoso instrumentalists. Altissimo register passages in the four solo parts (as in m. 32), glissandos (m. 328 ff.), and a variety of attacks and dynamic levels are some of the more formidable performance challenges. However, the endurance problems in the *Sonata* version have been mitigated by reassignment of some of the original soloists' material to other instruments in the *Concerto*.

Diatonic, linear writing prevails over chordal and chromatic constructions. Even the solo horns are more frequently put together in horizontal, contrapuntal textures, though often in a doubled pair. Much of the main thematic material evolves from the initial melodic idea introduced by the third horn at the beginning (Example 37a). The scalewise descent in the subordinate theme of the sonata-

Example 37.   *Concerto for Four Horns and Orchestra.*

a. first movement, mm. 3–7.

b. third movement. mm. 316–21.

form first movement (m. 49) derives from it as do segments of the main theme of the Adagio second movement at measures 216 and 229. Augmenting the cyclic effect of earlier musical material returning in later movements, the main theme of the Rondo finale has its source in the first movement (compare Examples 37a and b).

Chávez told Alfred Frankenstein that he wrote the piece "under the spell of one of those hysterical mass religious observances during which thousands of Mexicans make prolonged pilgrimages to Christian shrines set up where Aztec shrines once stood."[12] There is the unmistakable stark, mystical quality that turned up a few years later in *Sinfonía de Antígona*, suggested by the dark timbres, nontriadic harmonies, diatonic modality, and linear counterpoint. Whether the *Concerto* should be called a programmatic work on the strength of Frankenstein's statement is doubtful. But it is safe to reiterate what Aaron Copland wrote of the *Sonata*: that "it would be hard to imagine a more personal music . . . one in which the composer writes what he hears without compromising one iota with the public taste."[13]

Concerto for Piano with Orchestra

A grant from the John Simon Guggenheim Memorial Foundation in 1938 provided impetus and financial support for the composition of a piano concerto. The *Concerto for Piano with Orchestra* was completed in 1940, and was premiered by pianist Eugene List with the New York Philharmonic under the direction of Dimitri Mitropoulis on January 1, 1942.

Composed three years after *Sinfonía India*, the *Concerto* establishes a milestone in the development of the composer's personal style—the universalization of his Mexicanism. Otto Mayer-Serra has described this plateau as "the stage when the alien substances, whether of folk or European origin elaborated in countries with an ancient tradition, become transformed into original material [through] the composer's talent for manipulation by purely musical methods." He compares the *Concerto* with Falla's *Harpsichord Concerto* and Bartók's *Fifth Quartet* in the fact that "the folk base has become pure music as a result of personal treatment of the component elements."[14] *Sinfonía India* exemplified the composer's mastery of Mexican nationalism, which he later returned to from time to time; but another path, the universalization of national elements, becomes clearly apparent with the *Concerto*.

Gerard Béhague has identified some of the folk elements that are integrated in the *Concerto* as pentatonic and diatonic melody, repeated rhythmic and melodic motives, percussive treatment of the piano, and the relentless flow of note values of the basic rhythmic unit.[15] Other indigenous elements assimilated into the work are linear counterpoint, modality, nontertian harmonies, and hemiola rhythm.

In the introductory Largo of the first movement, combined sounds of the piano, harp, and celesta produce a Debussian *gamelan* effect; the pentatonic melody helps to reinforce this somewhat Impressionistic quality which soon dissipates. When the Largo returns at the end of the movement, the material is more thoroughly worked out and extended than in the introduction. The Allegro agitato, at measure 31, begins with a cantando counter melody in the first horn which accompanies the percussive gesture in the piano (Example 38). A hemiola overlay of 6/8 over the prevailing 3/4 meter intensifies the agitation.

A retransition to the reprise of the Allegro agitato material begins at measure 697. Here, the octave alternation on E in the piccolo brings to mind the end of the first movement of *Sinfonía No. 3* (1951). The steadily mounting buildup of interest from the barest resources demonstrates the composer's consummate skill at symphonic writing.

Example 38.   *Concerto for Piano with Orchestra*, first movement. mm. 31–34.

senza dedale

Merging piano and harp timbres offer another hint of Impressionism at the start of the Molto lento second movement, but this is offset by polychords, polytonality, and increased chromaticism to give an acid coloring to the middle movement as a whole. Dissonant harmonic and melodic effects are held in check by the use of expressive diatonic melodies derived from the first movement Largo, as in the solo horn at measure 1185, and another variant of it developed in the extended coda (m. 1203).

The final movement, Allegro non troppo, draws on thematic material of the first movement, as in the piano part at measure 1289, but a new Gershwinesque jazz rhythmic pattern, introduced at measure 1342, becomes the primary energizer in the rhythmically active, agitated ending. A rapidly descending Db major scale, harmonized in parallel ninths, alternates with the jazz pattern just mentioned in reaching a dramatic climax at the end of the thirty-three-minute opus.

Concerto for Violin and Orchestra

In the notes for the recording of his *Violin Concerto*[16] Chávez disclosed the particular fascination that the violin had held for him since childhood. While his early ambition to play the instrument was never fulfilled, his passionate interest in it remained. The knowledge of the violin he gained as an orchestral conductor and as a composer of symphonic and chamber music was joined with his affinity for the instrument when he received an unsolicited commission for a major work for violin and orchestra in 1947. The request came by letter from New York businessman Murray •D. Kirkwood whom the composer had not met. Chávez agreed to the commission, and, in fact, had already worked out some preliminary sketches for a violin concerto. He completed the *Concerto for Violin and Orchestra* in the summer of 1950, and introduced it with the National Symphony Orchestra of Mexico on February 29, 1952. The soloist was Viviane Bertolami, wife of Mr. Kirkwood. The United States premiere, by Henryk Szeryng and the New York Philharmonic, conducted by Leonard Bernstein, took place October 7, 1965.[17] Arthur Cohn, then director of serious music at Mills Music, Inc., initiated negotiations for this illustrious New York performance.[18]

The work is organized into nine broad sections; sections I through IV (Andante, Allegro moderato, Largo, and Scherzo) return in reverse order (as sections VI through IX) after a central cadenza (section V). The elaborate and demanding cadenza thus serves as the keystone of the large arch form. Nicolas Slonimsky has described this formal structure whimsically as an "equilibrated specular octad possessing a perfect chilarity."[19] The reversal in the order of returning musical material also foreshadows a similar, but less thoroughgoing treatment in the Finale of *Sinfonía No. 5* (1953).

Each major section is both expository and developmental, and, as the sections return after the cadenza at the midway point, development often takes the shape of vertical inversion. An example of this development by inversion can be seen by comparing, among several other such cases, the solo violin melody at number *73* in the first Largo with the corresponding position in the second Largo (no. *137*), where the inverted melody is played by English horn (Example 39). Inversion and normal order occur simultaneously in a few notable instances in the second half of the concerto: at *124*, where the Scherzo head motive and its inversion (or vertical mirroring) are joined in identical rhythm; and at *145* in the second Largo where the theme, played at a forte dynamic level by the solo violin in the low register, is reflected softly in a high inverted image by the first and second violins (García Morillo, 139).

Unlike the *Piano Concerto*, which is more fully scored, and which approaches what might be described as a symphony for piano and orchestra, the *Concerto for Violin* calls for a light orchestral accompaniment for the most part. The orchestral fabric is often reduced to soli passages; full tutti sections are minimal.

Example 39.   *Concerto for Violin and Orchestra.*
a. no. 73.

b. no. *137.*

© *Copyright 1964 by Mills Music, Inc. Used by permission of Belwin-Mills Publishing Corp.*

Concerto for Trombone and Orchestra

Like the *Violin Concerto,* the *Concerto for Trombone and Orchestra* came about through a particular person's wish to see an increase in the serious repertory for a specific solo instrument. In this case the interested party was Per Brevig, principal trombonist of the Metropolitan Opera Orchestra. In 1976 he approached Chávez about writing a concerto for the trombone. They agreed on terms (the fee was to be between three and four thousand dollars which Brevig would finance himself). Brevig demonstrated his range and technique for Chávez, and the composing began. Brevig admits to expecting a colorful tour de force on the order of a *Sinfonía índia* for the trombone. Chávez sent the score to Brevig a few pages at a time as they were finished; the opening cadenza contained the difficult pedal tones the trombonist had demonstrated earlier. As Chávez reached the midpoint in the work, Brevig commented to him that he was anxious to get to the "allegro," since the tempos to that point had been very slow, ranging between   ♩ = 40 and ♩ = 50. Finally, a Piu mosso (♩ = 72) containing virtuosic writing appeared in measure 73 and at later points.[20]

The *Concerto for Trombone* was completed in January of 1977. It was programmed at the Ninth Interamerican Festival in Washington, D.C., on May 9, 1978, with Chávez in his final conducting appearance. Rehearsal preparation of the *Trombone Concerto* went poorly. The slow sections almost stopped, according to Brevig, who points out that maintaining forward motion in these sections is a major performance obstacle. The performance went well despite Chávez's ill health (which seriously curtailed his conducting gestures). The piece was played again with Brevig as soloist by the Harmonien's orkester in Bergen, Norway, on October 11, 1979, with Enrique Bátiz conducting.

Chávez sought to exploit the sonorous capabilities of the trombone in the eighteen-minute, one-movement work. Open and muted timbres, glissandos, pedal and altissimo registers are all called into play, but also, unfamiliar mixtures of sonorities result from the many unison and octave doublings of the trombone with instruments like flute, oboe, and violins. Particularly attractive sounds issue from passages like the one for muted solo trombone and muted brass at measure 85, and the duet for oboe and solo trombone (in a whisper mute) at measure 25. Much of the melodic material for the solo instrument is severely disjunct, its angularity sometimes caused by octave displacement of adjacent chromatic notes. In fact, the piece is made up of a series of connected modules in which a segment of the chromatic scale becomes a repository of notes for the pitch material within the module. The soloist is challenged to negotiate extremely difficult series of melodic intervals, sometimes with great rapidity; an example of this appears in the Scherzando passage beginning in measure 194 (Example 40).

The *Concerto* belongs to those compositions since 1950 that are mainly nonrepetitive. But overall formal order can be seen in the placement of the two tuttis in the first third and last third of the piece. Strings are tacet in the middle portion, and the cantando (m. 27) and cantabile (m. 209) sections balance each other at the outer extremes of the broad design. The climax of the work is reached just before the Scherzando at measure 191. The ending, with sustained trills in the woodwinds and strings, has the effect of a continuation beyond the limits of the score. Brevig speculates that the composer may have thought of this work, the last major work he completed, as a kind of requiem. Whether or not this is true, the *Trombone Concerto* is an addition to the literature for an instrument whose modern solo repertory has long been in need of enrichment.

The symphonies and concertos are the most conservative of Chávez's orchestral works. But the conservatism rests in their bow to repetitive formal structures. They are models of innovation in the ways in which these forms are manipulated and in the substance of musical thought that generates their formal structure and derives from it. The more progressive leanings are to be found in the late orchestral works which, together with miscellaneous orchestral and band music, are discussed in the following chapter.

Example 40.   *Concerto for Trombone and Orchestra*, mm. 194–96.

6

The Late Orchestral Works;
Miscellaneous Orchestral and Band Music

The following discussion deals with three categories of works: transcriptions and arrangements for orchestra; music written for, or arranged for band; and the late (1964–1971) orchestral compositions. Chávez, who began writing for orchestra in his teens and for band in 1950 continued to produce music in both of these performance media in the later years. His *Trombone Concerto* was completed in early 1977, and he was well along with a cello concerto when he died. Between 1964 and 1971, he received commissions which accounted for the production of a half-dozen of his most experimental orchestral works. For band there are *Mañanas Mexicanas*, *Tintzuntzan* (both 1974), *Zandunga Serenade* (1976), and an arrangement of the orchestrally conceived *Chapultepec*.

Arrangements and Transcriptions
for Orchestra

Chávez made adaptations for orchestra of both music written by other composers and works of his own. In the first group are *Chaconne in E Minor by Dietrich Buxtehude* (1937) and the modern reorchestration of Antonio Vivaldi's *Concerto, Op. 6, No. 1*. Conversion of his own music for other media into versions for orchestra occurred with the transcription of *Llamadas*, written originally for chorus and orchestra in 1934. For its reworking as an orchestral piece in 1973, the composer retitled it *Paisajes Mexicanos*. The year 1935 witnessed the arrival of Chávez's orchestral arrangement of three traditional Mexican songs, originally entitled *Obertura Republicana* but later renamed *Chapultepec*. Finally, he scored Jaime Nunó's *Mexican National Hymn* for orchestra in 1941. The orchestral suites from the ballets *Horsepower* and *La Hija de Cólquide* will not be discussed in the present chapter; their music is addressed in Chapter 7—"Dramatic Works."

Chaconne in E Minor by Dietrich Buxtehude

Completed in September of 1937, the orchestration of *Chaconne in E Minor by Dietrich Buxtehude* was premiered by the Symphony Orchestra of Mexico on September 29, 1937, with Chávez conducting. In preparing the piece for publication in 1960, the composer made, at the suggestion of Arthur Cohn, a second version for small orchestra.[1] Chávez claimed that he was not trying to imitate the sound of the Baroque organ or a modern organ, but merely wished to acquaint audiences with Buxtehude's music.[2]

Buxtehude, the famous organist whom J. S. Bach journeyed two hundred miles on foot to hear in Lübeck, Germany, employed a standard Baroque variation procedure in this chaconne.[3] A four-measure repeated bass melody provides the musical bedrock for continuously flowing variations in the upper parts, usually in coupled pairs, on the implied harmony. As the twentieth (of thirty-one) appearance of the theme is reached, two successive chromatic bass melodies substitute for the prevailing diatonic bass theme. Example 41 shows the main diatonic bass melody and its two chromatic surrogates.

The composer took advantage of the opportunity to further vary the existing variations by a change in the ensemble makeup of each second member of the many coupled pairs. Almost without exception, the ensemble is varied every four measures. Octave doubling brings out the full range of orchestral colors, but tuttis are used sparingly until the climactic conclusion.

Characteristic organ figuration occurs at measures 69, 76, 97, and 105. These passages sound like an organ despite Chávez's intention not to imitate the instrument. Nevertheless, the piece is a masterful restatement of a Baroque musical monument in modern orchestral language. Colin McPhee described it as "simple, full-bodied, and eloquent, and worth comparing with the overgilded Bach arrangements of Stokowski."[4] Recently the piece has been used as an elegy to the composer in homage concerts dedicated to him.

Example 41.   *Chaconne in E Minor.*
a. mm. 6–9.

b. mm. 78–81.

c. mm. 90–93.

© *Copyright 1972. Used by permission of Associated Music Publishers, Inc.*

Concerto in G Minor,
Op. 6, No. 1 by Vivaldi

Another orchestral piece adapted from a Baroque musical source appeared in 1943. This setting is a reorchestration of *Antonio Vivaldi's Concerto in G Minor, Op. 6, No. 1* (=F. I n. 192) for violin, strings, and continuo.[5] The still unpublished work received several performances shortly after its completion; Chávez conducted it in Mexico City in 1943, 1944, and 1946, and in San Francisco in 1944. Its typical Vivaldi format has a stately Allegro first movement, an elegant Grave middle movement, and a bouncing Allegro finale. Thematic incipits from each movement are shown in Example 42.

In his review of the 1944 San Francisco performance, Alfred Frankenstein gave the work the following accolade:

Carlos Chávez conducted . . . a magnificent new orchestration by himself of a *Concerto Grosso* [sic] by Vivaldi. If the orchestral music of the eighteenth century must be recast in order to make it sound in the large concert halls of our time, that recasting should be done in this style, for Chávez does not attempt to romanticize the music or make it strut a bigger gesture than it naturally possesses; his Vivaldi remains Vivaldi, and does not become a cross between Rimsky-Korsakov and Strauss.[6]

Example 42.   *Concerto in G Minor, Op. 6, No. 1 by Vivaldi.*

a. first movement, mm. 1–3.

b. second movement, mm. 92–93.

c. third movement, mm. 116–19.

Chapultepec

Chapultepec, subtitled *Three Famous Mexican Pieces*, is an orchestral arrangement of three popular Mexican tunes. The opening "Zacatecas March" by Genaro Codina (1851–1901) is followed by "Vals Club Verde" by Rodolfo Campodónico (1866–1926), and the medley concludes with an anonymous Revolutionary song "Adelita." The piece was completed in October of 1935 and performed in the same month by Chávez's Mexican orchestra. A note attached to the score indicated, rather facetiously that the word *Obertura* [Overture] in its initial title did not have anything to do with the structure of the work, but that the composer "chose it because the sound of the word is pleasant."[7] The title was changed to *Chapultepec* at the suggestion of Arthur Cohn of Mills Music when the work was published by that firm in 1968.[8]

The march and waltz reflect the strong European influence on the cultural life of Mexico which culminated in the long regime (1876–1911) of President Porfirio Díaz. "Adelita" portrays a young *soldadera* in the Mexican Revolution of 1910. The lively and arrogant "Adelita," in its position at the end of the medley, alludes to the overthrow of the Díaz regime and what it stood for.

Rather than bedeck these little pieces in splendorous symphonic garb, Chávez set them as caricatures of how they must have sounded in countless town band concerts in Mexico. He exaggerated the more obvious band effects like high clarinets, brassy trumpets, and martial percussion. He also abetted his cause by adding four saxophones to the orchestra.

For the initial performance, Chávez wrote the following defense of this borrowing popular music for the concert hall.

I do not see why our audiences should be deprived of the beautiful melodies that I have combined into *Obertura Republicana*. I don't know how it turns out that our Republican music is not "highbrow" enough for symphonic treatment when this is not true of minuets and colonial masses . . . Nobody will doubt. on hearing these delightful melodies. Mexico's very own. that they belong to an epoch and a place. Here is the National music . . . [9]

Not surprisingly, the piece was programmed in the 1940 concerts of Mexican music presented by the Museum of Modern Art in New York. In 1947, it was given dance treatment by the Mexico City Ballet, with sets by José Clemente Orozco (García Morillo, 87).

Himno Nacional Mexicano de Jaime Nunó

In 1947, Chávez made an orchestral version of the spirited Mexican national anthem which was composed in 1853 by Jaime Nunó (1825–1908). Nunó's *National Hymn* had been the winning entry in a competition for a national anthem and was officially adopted on August 12, 1854.[10] Chávez's arrangement, which has remained unpublished, was performed by the Symphony Orchestra of Mexico during the seasons of 1941 to 1943.

Band Music

Chávez's first work for band was an arrangement of his orchestral triptych *Chapultepec*. The two versions were published in 1968 by Mills Music, Inc. Frank Ericson's band scoring of *Sinfonía India*, which was not authorized by the composer, has already been mentioned in the discussion of the symphony. Not until 1974 did Chávez write for band again; this time he once more transcribed an earlier composition of his own; it was a transcription of a transcription. In 1973 he scored his *Llamadas* (1934) for orchestra and called the orchestration *Paisajes Mexicanos* [Mexican Landscapes]. *Llamadas* in its original form was a "proletarian" symphony for chorus and orchestra. It was performed, with Chávez conducting, at the inauguration of the Palace of Fine Arts in Mexico City on September 2, 1934 (Artist Diego Rivera supplied illustrations for the performance). The band transcription of the orchestrally recast *Llamadas* was done in 1974 and received at least one performance in its complete form, with Chávez conducting the Goldman Band in New York.[11] It was later split into two parts, of which the first was given the title *Mañanas Mexicanas* [Mexican Mornings], *Symphonic Variations for Band; Mañanas* was published by Carl Fischer, Inc., in 1977. The second part, entitled *Tintzuntzan*, is being prepared for publication by Carl Fischer. The composer's final band piece, *Zandunga Serenade*, was written in 1976 for a series of school band compositions commissioned by Carl Fischer. Arthur Cohn, who, as head of serious music for Mills Music, Inc., had promoted the publication of so much of Chávez's work in the 1960s, moved to the Carl Fischer firm and continued to champion the printing of his music.[12]

Mañanas Mexicanas, Symphonic Variations for Band

Mañanas Mexicanas (1974) was performed by the Goldman Band at Damrosch Park in Lincoln Center on July 23, 1978, under the direction of Miguel Coelho.[13] Although in a deliberately Mexican style, the piece does not quote from folklore. Chávez wrote in his preface to the score that "the colors of the land, the scent of the orchids, and the accent of local speech make it relate to idiomatic expression."[14] In musical terms, melodic phrases harmonized in thirds, fourths, and sixths, and indigenous rhythms and instruments—marimba and güiro—generate an unmistakably "Mexican" flavor. Its themes, though original, echo familiar songs from Mexico.

Six interrelated themes correspond to the work's six main sections marked by contrasting tempos. A theme and one variation of it appear in each section, and the variation usually extends to serve as a bridge to the ensuing section. Subtle rhythmic, melodic, and harmonic changes obtain in the variations which are also treated with altered instrumentation and fragmentation among the variation devices used. Intermittent atonal or polytonal counterpoint spikes the diatonic themes and the predominantly pandiatonic accompaniment.

The beginning section is introductory in nature, partly because of the location, but also due to the heraldic opening fanfare in the brass. The theme is played by trumpets and horns harmonized in parallel thirds, and is accompanied by the lower brass in a different key (Example 43).

Example 43. *Mañanas Mexicanas*, mm. 11–14.

A repeat of the fanfare and the varied theme follow, but at a higher pitch level and with altered instrumentation.

Subsequent sections include a Scherzosamente, an Andantino (waltz), an Allegretto (stylized *mariachi* episode), a Calmo (slower waltz), and a Tempo di marcia. In typical *mariachi* fashion, the Allegretto 6/8 has pairs of three eighth notes each pitted against braces of two, and superimposition of duplets over the prevailing triple beat division. Twice in the section (mm. 148 and 180) Chávez inserts a five-note motive very similar to the beginning enunciation in *Tierra Mojada* (written two years earlier than *Llamadas*).

A fortissimo tutti transition leads to the final Tempo di marcia which opens with vamp in martial rhythm. Its theme comprises two contrasting ideas: a stiff melodic gesture at measure 251 (292 in the variation); and the cantabile at 264 (and 311). A raucous tutti transition ushers in the coda which capitalizes on the rhythmic vamp and first part of the theme from the march section. The final ten measures are new, that is, they were added to effect an ending for *Mañanas* at a point that was formerly the middle of *Paisajes*.

Zandunga Serenade

Zandunga Serenade (1976), written on a commission from Carl Fischer, Inc., for school bands, was published in 1977. It was programmed on the Goldman Band concert program in New York on July 23, 1978, conducted by Miguel Coelho, that also included *Mañanas Mexicanas.*

Just over three minutes in length, *Zandunga Serenade* is, like *Mañanas*, in a Mexican-engendered style without any quotation of actual folk music. A note in the score indicates that there is no conceived program, but that the piece "suggests the effect of tropical nights, the sound of trees in the light wind, with distant plaintivelike chants in the background." The moderate 6/8 meter established at the outset is maintained throughout the piece with only occasional ritardandos. But the flow of eighth notes is constant, and the previously cited two-versus-three rhythmic extensions of the meter keep it honestly Mexican. Sparse contrapuntal texture prevails.

The opening motive in the high woodwinds (which is also akin to the *Tierra Mojada*-like motive found in *Mañanas*) foreshadows the chief melodic motive of the piece found in the horns, alto clarinet, and saxophones at measure 8. Example 44 shows the latter motive (a) to be derived from the incipient announcement (b) at the beginning. There are several statements of the motive and other recognizable fragments of it; it is treated imitatively at measures 35 and 36. The motive in its embryonic state (at the beginning) returns at the end (mm. 59 and 73) but with a widening of its previously narrow pitch compass. A four-bar soli percussion passage leads to the tutti coda at measure 73.

Example 44. *Zandunga Serenade.*
a. mm. 8–9.   b. mm. 1–2.

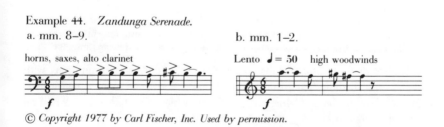

Brittle harmonies, especially those involving major sevenths and minor ninths, quartal and quintal chords, and unrelenting counterpoint keep the piece wholly in the Chávez idiom. Occasional harmonization in parallel thirds adds to its Mexicanism. In his moderation of technical difficulties in *Zandunga Serenade*, Chávez has afforded school band musicians a viable access to his music.

The Late Orchestral Works

The opening of Mexico's National Museum of Archeology in 1964 was an event of global significance. Probably never before has such a vast collection of prehistorical art and artifacts been more majestically exhibited. Fittingly, the country's leading composer was given the honor of composing the inaugural musical work. The inauguration took place on September 17, 1964, and with it came the world premiere of *Resonancias*. The piece was the first of six orchestral works he wrote between 1964 and 1971. In 1965, he fulfilled a commission from the *Südwestfunk* radio network in Baden-Baden with *Soli III* for bassoon, trumpet, timpani, and orchestra. *Elatio* was written in 1967, *Discovery* and *Clio* in 1969, and *Initium* in 1971. Chávez completed only two additional orchestral works: the still unpublished *Sonante* for string orchestra, and the *Concerto for Trombone*, available on rental from G. Schirmer, Inc., the firm that published a version of it for trombone and piano in 1982. All of these works were commissioned and all of them were written at a time when Chávez was virtually unencumbered with teaching and administrative responsibilities.

Resonancias

The Secretariat of Public Education commissioned the inaugural composition for the opening of the National Museum of Archeology. It was completed on July 28, 1964, at the composer's Cuernavaca residence, and he led the National Symphony Orchestra in its premiere at the inauguration. *Resonancias* [Resonances], a continuous fifteen-minute work, is mildly programmatic but without a specific program. Chávez described it as

a musical work more abstract than not, one which seems to encompass the manifold echoes that resound in me of an era that is past yet whose spirit is forever present in the immortal monuments of secular art and other manifestations as deep as they are dramatic . . .[15]

Chávez draws his impressions of this powerful and mysterious antiquity with chiaroscuro shadings The prominence of double reeds and low-pitched instruments (as in *Sinfonía de Antígona*) helps to achieve the dark coloring and an overall somber mood. As one might expect from its raison d'etre, *Resonancias* requires some indigenous percussion instruments; these include rasping sticks, güiros, and clay rattles. Exotic percussion effects abound. There is a unique cymbal soli (mm. 88–90) engaging all four percussionists, and a pianissimo combination of drum rolls (on twelve different drums) and tremolo lower strings that comes off in performance as sheer magic (m. 59ff.). Parsimony of ensemble is the rule, but rare mixtures of sound, like bass clarinet, violins, and violas (m. 255), dazzle the listener. An exceptional effect by a more traditional instrumental grouping is the "chirping" dovetailed woodwind passage shown in Example 45.

Example 45. *Resonancias*, m. 142.

Nicolas Slonimsky described *Resonancias* as "a polyphonic essay in ordered thematic resonances and rationally copulated dissonances in a *sui generis* technique in which melorhythmic patterns are never repeated."[16] The technique Slonimsky refers to in his hyperverbal statement is, obviously, the nonrepetitive procedure Chávez adhered to in most of his late works. A tape recording made for broadcast by George Szell conducting the Cleveland Symphony Orchestra in 1977 reveals just how resonant *Resonancias* can be. Regrettably, there is not yet a commercial recording of the work.

Elatio

In 1967, the Secretariat of Public Education once more issued Chávez a commission for an orchestra piece, this time for the Centennial of the Restoration of the Mexican Republic. He fulfilled the charge with *Elatio* [Exaltation] which he wrote during May and June of the same year; the commissioned performance occurred the following July 15, with the composer conducting the National Symphony Orchestra. He conducted the work again with the National Spanish Orchestra in Madrid at the Second Festival of American and Spanish Music on October 28, 1967.

The score, still in manuscript, was unavailable for the present study, nor could a recording of it be found. However, Chávez's notes for the piece are quoted in a March 9, 1969, program of the Little Orchestra Society in New York. He conducted both *Elatio* and *Toccata for Percussion* at this performance. His description of the novel organization, materials, and procedures he employed in *Elatio* will serve to give some insight into the work in absence of the score.

The music of this work follows a course from the low register to high. whence its name. This is a unit in which the orchestral depth. densities. and timbres are particular to each moment of the musical *processus* (no measure could be anywhere but where it is—before the next measure and after the preceding one). The depth, the density, and the timbric function here as architectonic constructive elements. By "depth" I mean the distance between the lowest and the highest notes at a given moment; by "density," as goes without saying, the larger or smaller number of instruments playing together; by "timbric," the manner in which the orchestral colors of the instruments are husbanded, combined, and contrasted. There is this particular about the atonal character of the piece: the tonal intervals *per se* (major third and its inversion, perfect fifth, fourth, and octave) have been almost completely dispensed with both melodically and harmonically. Repetitive and symmetrical constructions, too, are almost completely absent.

He instructs some of the players on points that shed light on his novelty and detail of orchestration. He tells the harp players to stand facing the pillar of the instrument in order to reach the lowest strings with both hands. To the percussion battery he clarifies the selection of drums for the piece.

(1) Percussion I: three pairs of *bongos* (small Afro-Cuban drums)—six different pitches—producing a continuously ascending scale, from low to high; (2) Percussion II: three snare drums—small, medium, and large—equivalent to high, medium, and low pitches respectively; (3) Percussion III: one tenor drum and two *congas* (elongated Afro-Cuban drums), the latter lower in pitch than the former; one *conga* lower in pitch than the other. Remark: the lowest *bongo* higher in pitch than the highest snare drum; the tenor drum lower than the lowest snare drum.

Elatio was not as well received in the New York performance as was the consistently audience-pleasing *Toccata for Percussion*, its companion work on the program. Critic Byron Belt acknowledged it as being, despite its severe atonality, an effective work in its intensity and colorful instrumentation, and one that is singularly the composer's own.[17]

Discovery

Discovery was commissioned by the Cabrillo Guild of Music and the Santa Cruz Bicentennial for the 1969 Cabrillo Music Festival. The composition was to commemorate the discovery of San Francisco Bay by Gaspar de Portola and his party who passed near Aptos, California, on October 16, 1969. Chávez completed the work on July 10, 1969, and it was premiered at the 1969 Cabrillo Festival. Its enthusiastic reception led to an invitation for Chávez to become musical director of the festival the next year. He accepted and included *Discovery*, which he conducted, on the 1970 program.

The twenty-minute work is scored for strings, a small complement of winds (flute doubling piccolo, oboe, English horn, clarinet, bassoon, two horns and trumpet), and percussion (playable by one percussionist). In his 1969 and 1970 Festival program notes, the composer examined the meaning of "discovery" in relating the piece to its commemorative origin.

All discoveries—I think—ought to be more or less substantially alike: there are elements of gestation, decision, search, strength, doubt, renewed strength, revelation, confidence

. . . Probably the discovery of lands was not much more different than the discovery of music is.

He applies the idea of discovery to his nonrepetitive technique: the thought that the act of discovery precludes repetition. He also admits to minimizing, in *Discovery*, the use of intervals that tend to establish and maintain tonality.[18] This evasion of tonality (or the resulting atonality), coupled with the predominantly linear texture, bespeaks Webern (a particularly Webernesque episode occurs in the pointillistic woodwind writing in measures 182–89).

The piece begins in the nether region of the strings—a soli for two double basses. They are then joined by solo cello, and the ensemble steadily mounts to envelop the entire string section. Strings, their density often increased by multiple divisis (up to a six-way division in the first violins, and a four-way division in the cellos), firmly anchor the piece; however, passages like the forty-five measure trio for horns and muted trumpet (mm. 191–235), the extended clarinet solo (mm. 76–103), and an oboe, English horn duet (mm. 104–13) tend toward the concertante idiom. An especially striking ensemble at measure 250 finds an insistent, sustained unison line in all of the woodwinds set against punctuating thrusts from the low-register strings (Example 46).

The piece ends in a flurry of fortissimo sextuplet sixteenth notes in the strings (divisi) and woodwinds leading to the trilled dodecaphonic final chord.

Example 46. *Discovery*; mm. 250–52.

Clio, Symphonic Ode

Ima Hogg, longtime patroness of the arts in Houston, commissioned Chávez to write a work for the Houston Symphony in 1969. He answered the commission with *Clio* which he completed on November 19, 1969; the Houston orchestra performed it on March 23 of the following year under the direction of Hans Schwieger.

Scored for full orchestra, including two harps and requiring four percussionists, the fifteen-minute work shows Chávez in full control of a highly complex mature orchestral style. He marshals his own personal brand of counterpoint, atonality, manipulation of dissonance, and orchestration into constantly renewing streams of "nonrepetition." Development takes the form of new, but related ideas spun off by their immediate antecedents within the major sections. A given texture, style, or ensemble is maintained long enough for the listener to perceive that a gesture has been both made, and to some extent developed. As in the other late orchestral works, there seems to be no limit in the composer's ability to turn up fresh, new sound mixtures in the ensembles. A case in point is the three-voice cantabile between solo flute, muted first violins, and a unison line in the horns, bassoons, and trombones (mm. 117–26.) which highlights one of the few, but impressive homophonic passages. Homophony also prevails in the choralelike section, harmonized mostly in fourths and fifths at measures 136 to 157, and at the beginning of the final section (m. 219). Here, the dissonant tension, charged with major sevenths and minor ninths, is kept at a remarkably consistent level (Example 47).

Example 47. *Clio*, mm. 219–22.

Initium

In commemoration of its twenty years of community service, the Witan Club of Akron, Ohio, commissioned *Initium* to celebrate the opening of the Edwin J. Thomas Performing Arts Hall. Chávez sketched the work in 1970, and scored it over the next two years. It was premiered by the Akron Symphony Orchestra, conducted by Louis Lane, on October 9, 1973. By prior agreement, Chávez gave the manuscript to the University of Akron for permanent display in Thomas Hall.

Initium's stated purpose was "to initiate the functions of a new hall dedicated to the cause of music and the performing arts . . ." As was his wont in describing his late, nonrepetitive works, Chávez wrote of shunning compositional formulas such as developments, imitation, ostinatos, orientalism, and the like.[19] The piece is continuous but sectional, and the sections divide into contrasting episodes. Chávez used a large orchestral palette—woodwinds in threes, vibraphone, xylophone, and marimba—in the eighteen-minute work, but drew from it economically; orchestral tuttis and large ensembles are infrequent, adding to their effectiveness when called upon. He calls for an extreme range of dynamics: *ff* is to be played as loudly as possible and *pp* as softly as possible.

Woodwinds begin with bold polyphonic gestures. The growing ensemble reaches ten players in multi-voice counterpoint at measure 15 where the linear statements are replete with nondiatonic scales and arpeggios, and polyrhythms. After a brief interlude by the vibraphone and another in the brass, woodwinds, and strings combine in a fourteen-voice polyphonic latticework (mm. 25–30). Though some voices duplicate the four or five concurrent rhythmic patterns, no voice duplicates the pitch pattern of any other part. The resulting chromatic atonality might be described as "panchromaticism" to distinguish it from the pandiatonicism so prevalent in Chávez's earlier music. Trilled chord clusters of major and minor seconds in the high woodwinds and strings, vibraphone, and glockenspiel effect a sense of suspended animation (mm. 41–45) in introducing the Lento section (m.47) with its unlikely dialogue between contrabassoon, horns, and double bass.

Pointillism—the rapid exchange of minute bits of melody between ensemble participants—takes over at the Animato section (m. 77). Winds, then strings, and later joined by four horns, finally slow the atonal leaping and bounding counterpoint to Lentissimo at measure 151. This central slow section is made up of a series of transparently scored episodes with varying instrumental colors and textures. The following section, Allegro, is announced with a snare drum roll and sustained high notes in the piccolo and flutes: this section is a progression of brass solis: horns and trumpets (m. 227); three trumpets (m. 233); horns, trombones, and tuba (m. 240); and finally, horns, trumpets, and trombones (m. 256). The trio of trumpets (mm. 233–37) is set in a type of homorhythmic counterpoint that is one of the earmarks of the composer: the rhythm is identical in each part, but the pitch patterns are different, thus a degree of melodic independence is achieved; and the resultant vertical sonorites, seemingly random, are carefully calculated and controlled to preserve a uniform harmonic quality (Example 48).

The concluding Lentamente, launched by fortissimo muted strings, ultimately receives full orchestral treatment, minus percussion, and ends fortissimo ("as

Example 48. *Initium*, m. 233.

loud as possible") on a G A C E chord whose consonance is destroyed by A# in the flutes and piccolo.

As impressive as the quantity of Chávez's orchestral music is its scope: symphonies of programmatic, nationalistic, romantic, and neoclassic nature; concertos for four different soloists or solo groups; new orchestrations of mid-Baroque and late Baroque music and arrangements of popular songs; and finally, the summing up of a most forward looking, mature abstract and personal style in the works since 1964. The band music is essentially utilitarian: rescored orchestral music; patriotic works; and music for school musicians.

7

Dramatic Works

When Mexican Secretary of Public Education José Vasconcelos commissioned Chávez to write a ballet on an Aztec theme in 1921, the illustrious career of one of this century's leading ballet composers began. Chávez composed five ballets between 1921 and 1968, and authored the scenarios of four of the five. As director of the Institute of Fine Arts from 1947 to 1952, and head of the Department of Dance within the Institute, he was in an ideal position to promote the creation and production of ballets; as previously mentioned, the dance art flourished in Mexico under his leadership.

The same ardor for literature which led Chávez into the areas of the solo song and choral music drew him also into the realm of the theater. His first effort in this direction was the composition of incidental music for a 1932 Mexican production of Jean Cocteau's *Antígone* adaptation. As *Sinfonía de Antígona*, the music he enlarged from the play has become one of his best known and most admired works. In 1947, Chávez was one of three composers to furnish music for Salvador Novo's production of *Don Quixote* (for the Fourth Cervantes Centennial); sharing in this joint venture were composers Blas Galindo and Jesús Bal y Gay. Chávez scored three scenes from the second act: "Ballet of the Lambs," "Windmills," and "Galley Slaves." The music for the first of these scenes was performed, under the title *Toccata for Orchestra*, by the National Symphony Orchestra of Mexico on July 22, 1947 (after its use with the play), conducted by the composer. Chávez provided incidental music for another Novo production in 1947: *Hippolytus* by Euripides. The music for this play, *Upingos* for solo oboe, like his earlier incidental music, has not been published.

Chávez wrote two dramatic works for soloists, chorus, and orchestra; they are the opera *The Visitors* (1953) and the cantata *Prometheus Bound* (1956). The following discussion will also include four compositions for chorus and orchestra which, though not cantatas in the strict sense of the word, are dramatic to a greater or lesser extent.

Ballets

Significantly, the first ballet Chávez composed, *El Fuego Nuevo,* was inspired by Aztec legend. It was to be the first of three ballets in which he drew upon the inherent dramatic wealth of ancient Aztec life and culture; *Los Cuatro Soles* (1925) and *Pirámide* (1968) are the other two. *Horsepower,* written in 1926, is also nationalistic, but in a modern sense inasmuch as it contrasts life in an industrial age with national tradition. Of his first three ballets, only the first was commissioned. All three were musical settings of scenarios written by the composer. In 1943, Chávez received his second ballet commission—from the Coolidge Foundation of the U.S. Library of Congress. Martha Graham supplied the plot for this ballet which bore the title *La Hija de Cólquide.* The composer's last ballet *Pirámide* was commissioned by Amalia Hernández for the Folkloric Ballet of Mexico. Completed in 1968, *Pirámide* has not yet been choreographed, and only portions of it have been performed in concert.

El Fuego Nuevo

Pedro Henríquez Ureña suggested to José Vasconcelos that Chávez be given the commission to compose a ballet on an Aztec theme in 1921. The resulting composition, *El Fuego Nuevo* [The New Fire] marked the beginning of the composer's Indian nationalism, but, moreover, it started a new era of nationalism in Mexican music. Nationalism since the revolution had been mostly urban centered—popular music firmly entrenched in European modes. In formulating his new style, the composer made no methodical study of Aztec music but relied on his own recollections of music of the Indians of Tlaxcala which he had heard since he was six years old. The new style was Indian in spirit—strong, sober, and laconic—but clearly his own; he rarely appropriated actual Indian melodies. One will observe, however, that part of the more obvious Indianism comes about through the persistent use of Aztec percussion instruments.

The first version of *El Fuego Nuevo,* for small orchestra, chorus of whistles, and women's chorus, was never performed. Vasconcelos's unsuccessful attempt to get an orchestral reading of the work by Julián Carillo has already been mentioned. It was first performed in concert in 1928 by Chávez's orchestra in a new mammoth orchestration which called for twenty-two woodwinds, eighteen brass, thirteen percussionists, strings, and women's chorus. The new version was repeated during the following two seasons of the Symphony Orchestra of Mexico, but has not been played since.

The plot is taken from an Aztec ceremony marking the end of a fifty-two year "century." The gods are implored to spare the people from a feared catastrophe; if the gods are merciful, there will be a renewal of life (another fifty-two years) through a new gift of fire. There are three main groups of dancers: warriors, priests, and women. The latter group moderates the violence of the warriors and the reverent serenity of the priests. The portent of gloom is portrayed with low instruments (bassoons and trombones) in the Prelude and again, similarly, in the Interlude between the Warriors' Dance and the Dance of Happiness. A germinal pentatonic motive binds together the various sections of the work. The lengthy percussion soli in the Dance of Terror is not only dramatically powerful, but historically significant by the fact that it presages Chávez's later music for percussion ensemble, *Toccata for Percussion* and *Tambuco*. The rondo finale, Dance of Happiness, captures the mood of overflowing jubilation at the awareness that the "renewal of life" has indeed been granted (García Morillo, 19–25).

For all of its brilliant staging potential and prophetic musical value, *El Fuego Nuevo* remains a youthful work. Chávez acknowledged it as such and did not press for its revival in later years.

Los Cuatro Soles

For his second ballet, *Los Cuatro Soles* (1925), Chávez again drew his source material from Aztec mythology. Four prehistoric paintings from the *Codex Vaticanus* depicting the destruction of the four *soles*, or epochs of Aztec life, were the composer's point of departure. According to legend, the first three epochs— water, wind, and fire—ended with floods, glacial wind, and fire respectively. The fourth epoch, earth, represents the present era which was believed would end with earthquakes.[1]

Written originally for small orchestra, soprano soloist, and women's chorus, *Los Cuatro Soles* was rescored for full orchestra before its premiere as a concert piece in 1930. Chávez led the Symphony Orchestra of Mexico in the 1930 performance and repeated it during the 1931 and 1935 seasons. Part of the small orchestra version—Prelude, Water Epoch, Interlude I, and Earth Epoch—was performed on programs sponsored by the Museum of Modern Art in New York in 1940. *Los Cuatro Soles* was not staged as a ballet until twenty-six years after it was written. This premiere took place on March 31, 1951, while the composer was director of the Department of Dance in the National Institute of Fine Arts in Mexico. Choreography was done by José Limón; Miguel Covarrubias designed the scenery and costumes, and José Pablo Moncayo directed the performance at the Palace of Fine Arts. Dancers were from the Mexican Academy of Dance and the School of Physical Education.

The Prelude and three Interludes are generally sparsely scored. They feature instrumental recitative and contrapuntal dialogue in contrasting instrumental colors. The Prelude begins with a pentatonic melody in the cellos and double basses which intertwines with solo oboe. In Interlude I, lower strings and clarinet oppose each other contrapuntally, and solo violin and horn do likewise in Interlude II. Unison women's chorus and soprano enter for the first time in the third Interlude. Subtle percussion punctuation helps to achieve an indigenous character in these more static sections of the work. Like *El Fuego Nuevo*, *Los Cuatro Soles* calls for native percussion instruments such as *teponaztles*, *huéhuetls*, Indian drum, *güiro*, water gourd, etc.

The music in the epochs themselves is, for the most part, denser in texture and rhythmically more dynamic than in the interludes. Persistent ostinatos add to the mounting agitation in the first three epochs as each progresses toward its catastrophic ending. In the fourth epoch Chávez used a preexisting Indian shepherds' dance which is so much in keeping with the rest of the melodic writing that it could pass for his own invention.[2] Example 49 shows the first three measures of this melody as Chávez set it symphonically in the original small orchestration.[3]

The chorus plays a prominent role in the final epoch which is a ritual dance to *Centéotl*, the goddess of corn. The vocal text simulates language but is in actuality pseudospeech, formed with syllables from the Aztec alphabet.

Polytonality is clearly present in many of the contrapuntal passages. Harmony in fourths and fifths and harsh dissonances, with brittle major sevenths and minor ninths, integrate in kaleidoscopic instrumental colors. *Los Cuatro Soles* marks the arrival of the mature composer, perfectly at home with the Mexican Indian nationalism introduced but not fully developed in *El Fuego Nuevo*.

Example 49.   *Los Cuatro Soles*, Epoch IV. beginning.

Used by permission of Anita Chávez.

Caballos de Vapor

Since the early 1920s, Chávez and painter Augustín Lazo had discussed the idea of a multi-media work which would project mechanization and its social implications in modern day Mexico. In the latter aspect, the music of the work would be an extension of "machine" compositions like Arthur Honegger's *Pacific 231* and

Sergei Prokofiev's *Pas d'acier.* Painter Diego Rivera and Chávez kept the idea alive, and it materialized in the "ballet symphony" *Caballos de Vapor* [Horse-power or H.P.], written between the years 1926 and 1932. In its final form, the work is in four movements; in that respect, and due to other formal considerations, it resembles a symphony (as its subtitle "ballet symphony" implies).

The fourth movement, for small orchestra, was composed first and was performed in New York's Aeolian Hall on November 28, 1926, at a concert of the International Composers Guild with Eugene Goosens conducting. The rest of the work gradually took shape over the next five years in a large orchestral format. It was premiered in a concert rendition by the Symphony Orchestra of Mexico on December 4, 1931. Leopold Stokowski examined the score when he was in Mexico to conduct that orchestra in 1931. He decided to program the work as a ballet in Philadelphia the following year. The widely publicized premiere of the ballet took place on March 31, 1932, under Stokowski's direction, and with stage direction by Wilhelm von Wymetal, Jr. Diego Rivera created the sets and costumes, and Catherine Littlefield provided choreography. It was danced by members of the Philadelphia Grand Opera Company, with Alexis Dolinoff and Dorothie Littlefield in the principal roles.

The plot, by the composer, contrasts the naturalness and sensuality of the tropics with invading northern industrialization and its attendant exploitation. Tropical climes are portrayed with native dances and dance rhythms like the *zandunga* (its original melody intact), the *huapango* (replete with duple-triple polyrhythms) and the alluring Argentine tango. The composer quotes from several *sones* ("tunes") of Mexican provenance in the fourth movement. In this movement, "Dance of the Men and Machines," he intermingles the industrial and exotic by juxtaposing the clamoring sounds of machines with bits and pieces of familiar Mexican melody. In the interlude to this movement he quotes the first four measures of the American popular song "Sidewalks of New York" (Example 50a), possibly to titillate the audience attending the 1926 premiere in the Gotham city. A motive derived from the *huapango* of the second movement also makes its way into the interlude (Example 50b). The *huapango* motive surfaced again in Chávez's 1932 choral composition *Tierra Mojada*, and in other later works.

The first movement, "Dance of the Man," is in a quasi-sonata form, or symphonic first movement form. The second, "Boat to the Tropics," consists of an "agile dance" and the *tango*, the latter for the luring of the sailors by a seductive sea siren. Standing in the usual position of the classical symphonic minuet is the third movement, entitled "The tropics"; its sonorous *huapango* and *zandunga* dances add credence to its being perceived as a symphonic third movement. Along with the machine music and quotations from Mexican tunes in the finale, the composer brings back material from the first movement to effect a

Example 50. *Los Caballos de Vapor,* fourth movement.
a. "Sidewalks of New York."   b. *huapango* motive.

motive

Used by permission of Boosey & Hawkes, Inc., and Anita Chávez.

cyclic symphonic unification of the whole work. The orchestration, which was somewhat reduced by the composer in 1954, features instrumentation underscoring modern Mexicanism: saxophones in the *tango;* marimba in the *huapango;* high clarinets and *mariachi*-like trumpets; and a percussion battery which includes *maracas, claves, güiro,* and small Indian drum.

Reviews of the ballet's premiere were, perhaps predictably mixed, but in general, the music stood up better in the critics' views than the realization of the scenario. Marc Blitzstein recorded the following observations after the initial performance.

I found the scenario of *H.P.* trite and unwedded to the score. Since Chávez' music is hard. not soft. literal. brutal and unperfumed. we were offered the paradox of a "Southern" composer dealing most successfully with the "Northern" aspects of his theme. The décors of Rivera were two-dimensional. like drawings. riotous in color. His costumes were good in their way. the way of a mummer's parade; enormous papier-maché pineapples. cocoanuts. bananas and palm-trees peopled the stage. the amiable product of a child's profuse imagination. They took up so much room that the logical choreographic plan should have been modelled on the simple *défilé;* instead of which. everybody was made to dance. the Big Fish got in the way of the Grand Pineapple. and the stage was invariably messy and ugly to look at.[4]

The first three movements of *Caballos de Vapor* were published in 1958 (incorporating the 1954 reorchestration) as *Suite de Caballos de Vapor.* Most modern orchestral performances and the two commercial recordings to date have preserved this reduced format. There is now, however, a recording by Eduardo Mata and the London Symphony Orchestra which includes the music for all four movements of the ballet.[5]

La Hija de Cólquide

Chávez's third ballet, *La Hija de Cólquide* [The Daughter of Colchis]. has nothing to do with Mexico past or present. Its plot revolves around characters from the ancient barbaric land of Colchis (Medea's land of origin). Martha Graham submitted her libretto to Chávez who, in 1943, was commissioned by the Elizabeth Sprague Coolidge Foundation to write the music. Instructed to write for a small orchestra for the sake of economy in production, he chose a double quartet of woodwinds (flute, oboe, clarinet, and bassoon) and string quartet. The music, which he sent to Graham in 1944, was set in nine sections.

As originally conceived, the ballet scenario presented four characters in a universal and timeless confrontation: Man is attracted to Woman, but elects to follow his Muse; Woman, who can be tender, becomes a witch when possessed by Fury, and in this state struggles to keep Man from the Muse; Woman ultimately gains control over Fury, becomes responsible and humanitarian, and is able to share Man with the Muse.[6]

The ballet was staged by Graham's troupe, with Graham herself as lead dancer, at the Plymouth Theatre in New York on January 23, 1946. By then the plot had been drastically altered and the title changed to *Dark Meadow*. The new scenario dealt with the human life cycle: the heroine is instructed by an earth mother and a personification of the male; a chorus of five women and four men strike archaic poses and stamp primitive dances in love imagery that connects fertility rites to human sexuality.[7] Martha Graham again mounted productions of *Dark Meadow* in New York in 1976 and 1977.

In 1946, Chávez extracted three sections from the ballet and designated them as *String Quartet No. 3*. He assembled the other six sections as *Suite for Double Quartet*, and, in 1946, he orchestrated five of these under the title *Suite Sinfónica de La Hija de Cólquide*. The symphonic suite was published in 1948 by Ediciones Mexicanas de Música, the composers' collective publishing firm Chávez helped to form in 1946. The suite was performed in both of the final two seasons (1947 and 1948) of the Symphony Orchestra of Mexico. The following diagram shows the derivation of the quartet and two suites from the ballet music.

Ballet		Str. Qt. III	Suite, Dbl. Qt.	Suite Sinfónica
I	Preludio	⟶	⟶	⟶
II	Allegro	⟶		
III	Lento	⟶		
IV	Allegro	⟶		
V	Interludio	⟶		
VI	Encantamiento	⟶		⟶
VII	Zarabanda	⟶		⟶
VIII	Pean	⟶		⟶
IX	Postludio	⟶		⟶

Since *La Hija de Cólquide* is best known in the form of the two suites, the following discussion addresses the structure of the orchestral suite in conjunction with the original scenario. The Preludio is like a potpourri overture in that most of its themes return in later movements; the Postludio is a compressed recapitulation of the Preludio, and the three reiterated themes appear in reverse order. The opening oboe soliloquy, in which the modal final G is alternated successively with other degrees of the modal scale (in the order of fifth, fourth, second, sixth, and third), returns to conclude the Postlude. The Preludio theme, starting at number *6*, comes back in the Postlude at *87* (Example 51a), and the Postlude's initial theme corresponds to the section in the Preludio beginning four measures before *14* (Example 51b). A three-note melodic motive in the closing section of the Preludio becomes thematic fodder for the Encantamiento movement, but its first descending second interval is frequently inverted to an upward seventh (Examples 51c and d).

Example 51.   *Suite Sinfónica de La Hija de Cólquide.*

a. Preludio no. 6.

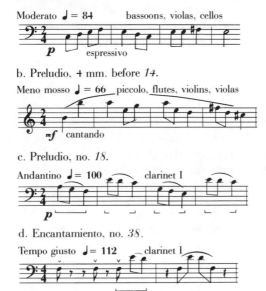

b. Preludio, + mm. before *14*.

c. Preludio, no. *18*.

d. Encantamiento, no. *38*.

The Daughter of Colchis (Woman) changes into a witch in the Encantamiento movement. There is an air of magic in the staccato syncopation, the suspended animation in the bass pedals, and the quiet background of motor rhythm. Mysticism rallies to a feverish pitch with Stravinsky-like brilliance in the ascending thirty-second-note scales and arpeggios played by high strings and woodwinds at the end of the movement. The Zarabanda is at the point in the scenario when the characters temporarily escape their conflicts by dancing. Serenity and exhilaration pervade the waltz (sarabande) and the lively 9/8 dance that follows it. The three-note motive that opens the movement (the pitches C. B, and E) is, according to the composer, a veiled dedication to Carl B. Engles of G. Schirmer, Inc.[8] The three-note figure from the Preludio (Example 51c) is also prominent in the Zarabanda; the movement is crowned with a bucolic final cadence in C major.

The Pean presents Woman's struggle for understanding and humanity. It is the most severe and desolate of the movements. Basically a variation rondo (ABA′B′A″), the movement borrows the motive for its secondary theme B (number 72) from the Preludio (one measure before 30). The grand climax of the Pean and of the suite arrives with a fortissimo tutti at B′ (number 81) of the rondo. The Postludio sees the characters united in tranquility.

The five-movement suite is remarkable for its overall musical integration, cohesion, and balance, especially when one considers that it is made up of pieces extracted from a larger work.

Pirámide

Pirámide [Pyramid], Chávez's final ballet and his third on an Aztec theme, was written in 1968. It was commissioned by Amalia Hernández, director of the Folkloric Ballet of Mexico. It was projected to be performed by that company, but to date has not been choreographed, and the music has yet to be played in its entirety in concert. The plot, by the composer, is summarized in his own words as follows.

This ballet is a fantasy in which are presented choreographic compositions. plastic. dynamic ensembles. primitive forms of life. and dances proper to suggest the passing of the human race from chaos. myths. superstitions. discoveries. etc.. to an ideal reunion and cooperation of people of all places . . .

I have portrayed a stylization of wind. water, earth, and fire personified in the Aztec gods and goddesses of these elements. leading to a struggle of primitive man. the discovery of fire. the development of architecture (symbolized by the building of a pyramid). and the getting together of men and women of all epochs and places. dressed in all sorts of costumes. dancing the final general dance.[9]

The ballet is in four acts: I. Chaos; II. The Gods; III. The Elements; and IV. The Men. Chaos is totally electronic, a magnetic tape of synthesized sounds.[10] Acts II and III—The Gods, and The Elements—are orchestral. Act IV, The Men, is for orchestra and chorus, the latter singing and speaking nonword syllables in a way reminiscent of *Los Cuatro Soles,* but with considerably more intricacy than in the earlier work. One a cappella chorus is in strict rhythmic speech (but not *Sprechstimme,* the half-sung, half-spoken technique employed often in twentieth-century music). In this chorus, published by Carl Fischer, Inc., as

Fragmento, the bottom and top lines of the musical staff represent the lowest and highest natural speaking voice; notes in between stand for gradations within these two extremes. The effects are strong, primitive, and emotionally expressive. The choral and orchestral strands are woven together into provocative textures and colors throughout most of the fourth act. But Act III, The Elements, is perhaps the most lucid in terms of orchestral tone painting; deft husbanding of pitch and timbre makes the elements as vivid as imaginable in a modern score. Especially noteworthy in the orchestral portions heard by this writer (Acts III and IV) is the prominence of low-range instruments such as tuba, bass clarinet, and contrabassoon, often plumbing the depths of their darkest hues in solo and soli passages. The inclusion of piano in the score marks one of the few times, and only in the late orchestral works, in which Chávez used the instrument to expand the timbral resources of the percussion section.

Act III was performed at the 1972 Cabrillo Music Festival, and the choral *Fragmento* from Act IV was premiered on the 1973 Festival program. The complete work is being investigated by Miguel Coelho in a doctoral study at New York University. He is reconciling the existing manuscripts in preparation of a new critical edition of the ballet.[11] He will also edit an orchestral suite from the ballet for publication by Carl Fischer, Inc.

Choral Works with Orchestra

Chávez's compositions for orchestra and chorus, in addition to the aforementioned ballets incorporating chorus, are *El Sol* and *Llamadas,* both written in 1934, an arrangement of the traditional song *La Paloma Azul* (1940), and *Canto a la Tierra* (1946).[12] The first two were written while Chávez was director of the National Conservatory of Mexico, and the second of these, *Llamadas,* was performed in the dedication concert of the Palace of Fine Arts on September 29, 1934, with the composer conducting the Symphony Orchestra of Mexico and a chorus from the Conservatory and the Night School of Art for Workers. Subtitled Proletarian Symphony, *Llamadas* [Calls], is a setting of verses from the Ballad of the Revolution, opening with the phrase, "This is how the Revolution will come!'" The work had been introduced earlier in the *Casa del Pueblo* at workers' union meetings, and its inclusion on the Palace of Fine Arts inaugural program was at the request of the workers.[13] Chávez made instrumental arrangements of *Llamadas* for orchestra (as *Paisajes*) and band (see *Mañanas Mexicanas*) in the 1970s.

The arrangement of *La Paloma Azul* was occasioned by the May, 1940 concerts in the Museum of Modern Art in New York where it was performed along with other selected works by Mexican composers. Secretary of Agriculture Marte

R. Gómez commissioned *Canto a la Tierra* which exists in, besides its form for unison chorus and orchestra, two other versions: unison chorus and piano; and unison chorus and brass ensemble of two horns, two trumpets, two trombones, and tuba. The five-minute work on a text by Enrique González Martínez has not yet been published.

El Sol

El Sol, Corrido Mexicano [The Sun, Mexican Ballad] was composed to a poetic text that is an optimistic paraphrase by Carlos Gutiérrez Cruz of a popular Mexican *corrido*. The initial quatrain of the original poem reads:

> Sun round and red.
> Like a copper coin.
> Daily you look at me.
> And daily you see me poor.

The text speaks of an appreciation of nature, but also alludes to the injustices to workers in Mexico's *haciendas*. All of the music is the composer's own except the melody used for the final four verses of poetry. Chávez's stated objective in *El Sol* (and also in *Llamadas*) was to write, as he directed young composers (his conservatory pupils) to write, music that was "simple and noble, and at the same time of high quality, in Mexican style which would take the place of vulgar commercialism" (García Morillo, 83).

Written for amateur chorus, *El Sol* illustrates the noble simplicity Chávez aimed for in its mostly homophonic textures and direct rhythms. The introduction begins with a modified version in the winds of the music used for the final four of the eleven poetic verses. Woodwinds and strings then set the pace and mood for the first quatrain: "O you red headed sun my golden shiner," in animated two-voice counterpoint (at no. *1*). At the words "*tierra mojada*" ("wet earth"), Chávez inserts a melodic motive which, as already cited, has found its way into several of his compositions. On the same words, it was the opening of the 1932 choral piece *Tierra Mojada*. This motive becomes the chief unifying element in *El Sol*, returning at numbers *22, 23, 27, 31*, and extended into a "mocking" theme at *38* (the latter being the same form of it found in the third and fourth symphonies). The final theme, in F major, begins at number *33*. It is the borrowed melody on which the first part of the introduction is based. This simple but powerfully dramatic theme (Example 52) underscores an open adoration of the sun.

An abrupt (one-chord) modulation at number *40* shifts the theme to Bb major. Repeating the same text seen in Example 52, the melody acts as refrainlike coda to the whole work. The piece ends on two jubilant Bb major chords (with added sixth, and an F bass) to the word "Sun," answering a similar treatment at

116   CARLOS CHÁVEZ

Example 52. *El Sol*, no. *33.*

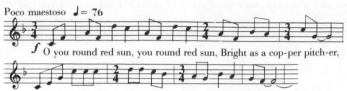

Poco maestoso ♩ = 76

f O you round red sun, you round red sun, Bright as a cop-per pitch-er,

Ev'-ry day you light the fields, And help to make the brown earth rich-er.

© *Copyright 1962 by Mills Music, Inc. Used by permission of Belwin-Mills Music Publishing Corp.*

number *13* (in F major). The choral sections and intervening instrumental episodes are liberally seasoned with Mexican spices. Melodies harmonized in thirds and *mariachi*-like manipulation of juxtaposed 2/4, 3/4, and 6/8 meters are as authentically Mexican as *jalapeño* peppers.

El Sol was premiered at a concert in the San Angel suburb of Mexico City on July 17, 1934, with the composer conducting the Symphony Orchestra of Mexico and the Conservatory chorus. His arrangement of the work for chorus and band (1934) was published in 1962, the same year as the choral-orchestral version.

La Paloma Azul

One of the four works Chávez contributed for the 1940 concerts of Mexican music at the Museum of Modern Art in New York was his arrangement of the popular *canción* "La Paloma Azul" [The Blue Dove] for chorus and small orchestra. This nineteenth-century *Canción* ("song") may have come to Mexico from Spain. Chávez, however, believed that it derived from some forgotten Italian opera aria, a remnant of a Mexican era in which European music was dominant. For the arrangement, Chávez used phrases from "La Paloma Azul" as well as bits of other popular Mexican songs. The text is the monologue of a lover who is departing for the northern Mexican town of Laredo and is saying goodby to his sweetheart. Intermittently, the *canción* breaks into a varied refrain with the words,

> What a beautiful blue dove.
> Don't have much to do with anyone.
> Open your wings.
> I am the keeper of your love.[14]

Suave harmony in thirds is assigned to alternating pairs of voice parts—sopranos and altos, and tenors and basses. Occasionally the pairs join in octave doublings, and less often in four-part harmony. The orchestra is more acid;

dissonances, some the result of ostinato chordal accompaniment, lend contemporary and personal stylization to the traditional strains of melody and their simple harmonization. The orchestral introduction and interlude (no. *24*) both contain fragments of the song phrases harmonized with paralled triads. Two guitars add a splash of *mariachi* to the petite ensemble, reinforcing the vocal rhythm with strummed chords. The "La Paloma Azul" melody itself, in 7/8 meter, is a graceful, floating air of unmistakable Mexican visage (Example 53). It reveals itself as the same tune Aaron Copland worked into his orchestral suite *El Salón México* (1936).

The piece ends in a quadruple reprise, with concomitant dynamic level reductions, of the first part of the melodic phrase seen in Example 53, to the words, "I come to bid you farewell."

Example 53.   *La Paloma Azul, no. 36.*

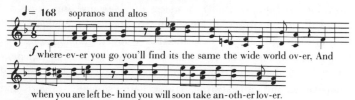

where-ev-er you go you'll find its the same the wide world ov-er, And

when you are left be-hind you will soon take an-oth-er lov-er.

Cantata and Opera

The year after Chávez's departure from the National Institute of Fine Arts was highly productive in terms of composition. In that year, 1953, he completed his third, fourth, and fifth symphonies. His next creative undertaking, an opera ultimately entitled *The Visitors*, took four years to complete. One other new composition appeared during those four years—*Prometheus Bound* (1956), the only composition he labelled a cantata. Neither of these two dramatic works has been published, and neither has been performed extensively: the cantata only once (in 1972); and the opera in three different complete productions between 1957 and 1963. Chávez's ongoing struggle for success with the opera brought it only a moderate amount of critical acclaim and little popular acceptance.

Prometheus Bound

Chávez began in 1956 to think of the practical problems of writing a cantata on *Prometheus*, a subject he had long believed would serve him well in a dramatic work. A John Simon Guggenheim Foundation grant he received that year freed some time to devote to this undertaking. He decided on R. C. Trevelyan's English translation of the Aeschylus tragedy (Cambridge: The University Press, 1939) because of its directness and simplicity of text, the beauty of its poetic images, and its rhythmic sense. He then set out to distil Trevelyan's text into a libretto which would preserve the essence and continuity of its original form. The finished work is a twenty-minute cantata for chorus, soprano soloist, and orchestra in a powerful contemporary idiom.

Prometheus is the "forethinker, the kind god who champions mankind, protects the feeble, and who heroically rebels against tyranny and injustice."[15] He is bound to the rocks by Power and Hephaistos, agents of the tyrannical god Zeus. Prometheus gives Io the troubling news that she will marry Zeus and will bear him a son who will free Prometheus from the evil god's forces.

Chávez contrasts spoken recitative, for the characters Power, Hephastos, the Chorus Leader, Hermes, and the Caller (who sets the scene and announces the stage rubric), with sung choruses of tenors and basses for Prometheus, and sopranos and altos for the Chorus. Io is the only character having sung solo dialogue. In most of the choral sections, Chávez wrote two melodically independent voice parts with the same rhythm and accompanying light orchestral doubling, punctuation, and underscoring. The orchestra similarly supports and links the phrases in spoken recitative. Dramatic expression peaks at Io's delirious soliloquy, at the point when she becomes aware of the role she must play to effect Prometheus' release. The solo soprano and accompaniment grow wildly agitated in the musical portrayal of Io's trauma. But the dramatic climax arrives with the final speech by Prometheus, this time sung by full SATB chorus. Full orchestra completes the massive, animated ensemble as the hero is tested by all the earthly furies Zeus unleashes upon him.

Prometheus Bound received its world premiere at the Cabrillo Music Festival in Aptos, California, on August 27, 1972. Chávez conducted the Festival orchestra and members of the Oakland Symphony Chamber Chorus in this performance. Soloists were Marian Marsh, sporano, and readers Willene Gunn, Dudley Knight, Jerry Walter, and William Hinshaw, III.[16]

The Visitors

In 1953, Lincoln Kirstein, director of the New York City Center of Music and Drama, asked Chávez to convey his ideas for an opera to poet Chester Kallman (who, with W. H. Auden had coauthored the libretto of Stravinsky's *The Rake's Progress*). The plan agreed upon by Kallman and Chávez was approved, and composition of the opera was commissioned jointly by Kirstein and the Rockefeller Foundation. Chávez completed the work four years later in 1956. It was produced by the Columbia Theater Association, Milton Smith director, in nine performances between May 9 and 18, 1957, at Columbia University's Brander Matthews Theater. Howard Shanet conducted.[17]

The title of the opera at the time of the New York production was *Panfilo and Lauretta*. Its plot deals with a group of four fourteenth-century Italian aristocrats who have sought refuge from the plague in a villa near Florence. To pass the time they enact little plays which somewhat fit their own personalities and interactions. Dioneo, a poet, is the play producer and catalyst of the group. Panfilo, a soldier, vies for the love of the young Lauretta who in her own vanity is aloof to his attentions. The older Elissa, former mistress of Panfilo, is at first jealous of Lauretta, but gradually reveals her capacity for understanding.

The little plays touch on both pagan and Christian themes. The first one, *Cupid and Psyche*, offers Panfilo and Lauretta the chance to play out their courtship, and for Elissa (as Venus) to intervene. The drama aborts when the actors' real-life situations conflict with the script. In the second play Panfilo, as a Roman centurion, ravishes Lauretta who plays the title role of Mary Magdalene. Panfilo and Lauretta personify Adam and Eve in the next enactment, and at Adam's downfall, a mob of rabble, infested by the pestilence, is let into the courtyard of the villa by a monk whom the would-be actors had earlier taken into their fold. Lauretta is stricken with the plague, and Panfilo leaves the villa.

In Act III, Lauretta, pregnant with Panfilo's child and recovered from her illness, forgives her beleaguered lover who has returned from the city to report that the pestilence is still raging. Reconciliation of the group comes about through completion of the *Cupid and Psyche* play, ordered by Dioneo. In the play's conclusion, the forgiving Venus (Elissa) announces that Psyche (Lauretta) has, through her suffering, propitiated love, and crowns her with a wreath of myrtle as a symbol of immortality.

The plays within a play afford a penetrating look at the characters and their interworkings through several different prisms. Sensitive musical scene painting is accomplished with judicious deployment of the full orchestral resources. Despite the composer's predilection for dissonance, the vocal melodies are eminently singable. Among the suavely lyrical arias are "Lazarus I Am," sung by the monk in Act II, and Elissa's large aria in her portrayal of Venus just before the finale. The arias tend to be static under which the orchestral accompaniment provides the dramatic movement. The chorus sets the opening scene and is otherwise used for the Latin dirge of the burial procession, and for the pestilent crowd. Solo ensembles are especially well turned, notably in the finales of the second and third acts, and in the laughing scene in Act II. The latter is treated as an extended a capella madrigal (Example 54).

Panfilo and Lauretta did not receive the critical acceptance Chávez had hoped for in New York. The opera was staged in a production by Salvador Novo in

Example 54.   *The Visitors*, Act II, laughing madrigal.

Used by permission of Carl Fischer, Inc.

Mexico City on October 28 and 30, and November 9, 1959, as *Love Propitiated*. With its tightened libretto, a new, larger orchestration, and a professional cast, the opera was a critical success.[18] Chávez revised the work again for another production in Mexico City, this time with a Spanish translation of the libretto, on May 21 and 25, 1963, and the reviews were glowing. Excerpts from the opera, again revised and retitled *The Visitors*, were performed in concert at the 1973 Cabrillo Music Festival in Aptos, California, with the composer conducting.[19]

Chávez took more pains with, and expended more energy on the opera than anything else he wrote. He revised the work for each subsequent production after its premiere and was two-thirds through with a final reorchestration when he died. In the 1970s he made a demonstration recording of excerpts to promote possible production of the work in New York and Boston. He also had a German translation made of the libretto in the hope of a European performance. Arthur Cohn believes that the opera never overcame the reviews of its New York debut. He tried to convince Chávez that the success of the Mexico performance was ample proof of its artistic merit.[20] Obviously not satisfied with this argument, Chávez devoted his final creative efforts to the opera.

Of all of his dramatic music, that part that Chávez provided for two of his ballets has become the most universally accepted. This is due in large measure to the suites he extracted from those ballets—*Horsepower* and *La Hija de Cólquide*. It is music that stands well on its own, but which is vividly enhanced by the scenario through which each suite is converted into highly pictorial programmatic music.

His efforts at gaining an enduring audience for his opera and oratorio remained frustrated.

8

Summary and Conclusion

San Francisco art critic Alfred Frankenstein appraised Chávez as "the most remarkable man I know." "Thanks to him," he wrote, "Mexico and all of Latin America have been placed on the musical map of the world . . ."[1] Chávez's roles as composer, conductor, teacher, lecturer, writer, and administrator earned him the reputation as the chief animator of music in Mexico in this century. Moreover, the wide dissemination of his music, and his musical statesmanship have revealed him as an international figure and a true artistic ambassador of his country.[2] Antonio Castro Leal attributes this success partly to the fact that Chávez came from a family of "battlers."[3] There can be little question of the enormous and consistent drive which enabled him to overcome obstacles that could have stopped someone less determined. His energy, creative talent, and organizational skill came to bear at a time in Mexico that was ripe for artistic growth and change—the end of the Revolution of 1910. This climate of rebirth was the crucible that forged a dynamic personality, one that shaped Mexican musical life for half a century and made the name Chávez synonymous with music in the Mexican Republic. Even today in Mexico one speaks of the periods in music "before and after Chávez." Although his name is still at the center of musical polemics in Mexico, it nevertheless remains at "the apex of the important search to invent a national tradition."[4]

The following discussion turns to a summation of Chávez's achievements in several spheres of activity in an attempt to arrive at a profile of the artist and the man.

Chávez the Composer

Chávez always considered himself primarily a composer, and he viewed his other endeavors as no more than a means of furthering his main calling. His musical creativity first surfaced at about nine years of age when he began to compose on his own concurrently with his first study of the piano. He was fortunate to have come into contact with accomplished musicians like Manuel Ponce and Luis Ogazón who helped to formulate his musical taste by acquainting the young musician with the best music of the past (Ponce) and the new musical currents in Europe (Ogazón). Ponce also encouraged him in the direction of musical nationalism, to which the older composer was giving nominal service. Harmony study was guided by Manuel B. Fuentes, but Chávez sought out the writings of the traditional theorists on his own, only to dismiss what he found in them to be empty academism, rigidity, and impracticality. Neither would he subject himself to the lengthy and ossified composition curriculum then firmly entrenched in the National Conservatory.

His earliest compositions were written mostly for piano or voice and piano in an apprenticelike emulation of the music he studied and heard around him. He also had a penchant for free improvisation, giving vent to spontaneous surges of experimentation which expanded his musical thinking. An observation trip to the musical centers of Europe in the early 1920s did little to alter the direction of a musical style which had by then struck paths into Mexican Indianism, and a personal extension of contemporary styles (Impressionism and post-Impressionism) already encountered in youthful explorations. An extended sojourn to New York (1926–28) brought contact with leaders of the musical avant garde like Copland, Varèse, and Cowell, and with the new American and European music being performed in concerts sponsored by the League of Composers and the International Composers Guild. This period marked Chávez's arrival as a mature composer, acknowledged as such by at least an elite group of cognoscenti, and promising the wider acceptance which followed.

Composition Style

Three broad stylistic tendencies are discernible in Chávez's mature musical output: first, Mexican nationalism; second, a complex of brittle dissonance, angular melody, atonality, and polyrhythm; and third, a more conservative style leaning toward traditional formal structures, moderation of dissonance, and tonality. The three are not mutually exclusive, and varying mixtures of them can be found in almost any work in question. Chávez was an inveterate contrapuntalist whose predilection for horizontally organized textures affected practically everything he wrote. Imitation, canon, and fugue crop up from time to time, but more often the counterpoint is of the free linear type with either pandiatonic, polytonal, or atonal orientation. One particular hallmark of his contrapuntalism is the homorhythmic combining of two or more melodically independent lines which come together to form seemingly random vertical sonorities. In works that are free of Mexican or Indian influences, he preferred, as a rule, melodic and vertical intervals such as seconds, sevenths, and ninths, which evade crystallization into a single tonality, and harmonies that fall outside of triadic construction. The latter includes melodic harmonization in parallel fourths and fifths, and the simultaneous use of adjacent notes of the chromatic scale in octave displacement, producing flint-hard chords charged with major sevenths and minor ninths.

In matters of rhythm, Chávez showed himself to be a careful craftsman and a bold experimenter who was able to create and deliver a rhythmic ambience appropriate to his compositional intentions. His music is characterized by frequent tempo changes indicated with both precise metronome markings and Italian rubric. Rhythmic vitality pervades his entire production, but it is most active when it takes the form of motor rhythm in an incessant, driving force of unbridled forward motion. He emancipated his music from the "tyranny of the barline" by placing accents on weaker pulses and by frequent shifts of meter. Polyrhythms, in which different beat divisions are superimposed—four against five, five against six, or even eleven against twelve—are not uncommon. But the most prevalent rhythmic gestures are those that are indigenous to Mexican popular song and dance: the three-duplet versus two-triplet arrangement in 6/8 meter; the substitution of a duplet for a triplet or vice-versa; and 5/8 or 7/8 meter organized in groups of two and three eighth notes. These rhythms abound in compositions alluding to modern day Mexico (as do melodies harmonized in parallel thirds and sixths), but they turn up to a lesser extent in the composer's absolute and Indianesque music as kind of a running current of style. Jazz rhythms appear rarely, but are quite conspicuous when present.

The synthesized Aztec style Chávez began to use in 1921 with *El Fuego Nuevo* results from an amalgamation of several ingredients: ostinato repetition of short melorhythms; modal and pentatonic scales; spare contrapuntal textures; brutish dissonance; and the use of native percussion instruments. Quotation of authentic Mexican Indian melodies, as in *Sinfonía India* and *Los Cuatro Soles*, is the exception to the usual practice of inventing new neoprimitive-sounding melody in such pieces.

"Nonrepetition," initiated in 1933 with *Soli I*, became a regular constructive feature from 1958 with the appearance of *Invención* for piano. The premise of nonrepetition is that music should unfold in a continual stream of new ideas. Each idea is generated by its antecedent idea and becomes the generator of the next. As in Hegel's concept that thesis and antithesis produce a new thesis, a constant process of renewal takes place. Continuity results from the direct relationship of each idea to its immediate forebear and descendent, and by the fact that moderate recurrence of material (in opposition to the basic tenet) is sometimes admitted into the otherwise nonrepeating structure. Though Chávez did not turn to this method of through-composition exclusively, he did use it for most of his progressive compositions of the 1960s and 1970s—especially the last three *Solis*, *Inventions II* and *III*, and in the late orchestral works.

A disdain of formulas, in favor of instinct based on experience, led Chávez to his nonrepetitive procedure and, for the most part, steered him away from the composition technique which attracted so many of his contemporaries— serialism. His bow to twelve-tone serial technique in the Aria movement of *Soli II* for woodwind quintet is one notable exception. In fact, twelve-tone technique permeates the entire movement. The "theme" of the *Theme and Variations for Violin and Piano* was also observed to be serial—a forty-two-note pitch series of which the last twenty-one notes are a retrograde of the first twenty-one. One would guess that other serial movements or passages might be hidden away in the nominally nonrepetitive works where chromatic-scale pitch equality is the rule. In any event, Chávez demonstrated that he could handle the Viennese method.

The four *Solis* embody a principle in which a group of solo instruments serve as a soli ensemble, and in which each instrument retains its own soloistic character within the group. *Solis I*, *II*, and *IV* are for small chamber ensembles, but the "soli" principle tends toward the concerto grosso model in *Soli III* where the soli group is given an orchestral backdrop. *Soli III* is thus akin to a symphony concertante, but with greater individuality on the part of each soloist.

An inseparable part of Chávez's compositional skill was his ability as an orchestrator. One is reminded of other conductor-composers in the twentieth century—namely Richard Strauss and Gustav Mahler—who were known particularly for their brilliant orchestration. As an orchestra conductor for fifty years, Chávez was intimately acquainted with instrumental colorings employed by other composers past and present, and he knew from first-hand experience the possibilities and limitations of orchestral resources. The acumen gained from this vantage point joined with fertile imagination and artistry to produce novel instrumental usages, and new hues and shadings. The most dissonant and intricate passages were made to "sound" by means of the right combinations of timbre and dynamics.

Chávez favored five-way writing in the string section with double basses independent of the cellos. Divisi scoring often expands the strings by a few to several independent parts. Double bass serves as both a solo and soli instrument in addition to its sectional role; in this respect it becomes almost an equal partner with its upper string counterparts. Lower-voiced instruments in the woodwinds and brass sections are given the same special consideration. Tuba, bass clarinet, and contrabassoon are used in a soloistic capacity with moderate frequency. Miguel Coelho recalls Chávez's complaint that there were not enough low instruments in the orchestra.[5] Perhaps the most striking facet of Chávez's orchestration is his seemingly inexhaustible supply of new soli combinations—small groups which contrast unique combinations of color and lightened density to the larger ensemble.

Toccata for Percussion and *Tambuco* have found their place in the permanent repertory of the modern percussion ensemble. In fact, the former work was a pioneering achievement in legitimatizing percussion ensemble performance. Chávez also proved how successfully percussion and small wind ensemble could be united with *Xochipilli*. No less interest or care in writing for percussion is seen in his works for orchestra. The orchestral scores seldom call for fewer than three percussionists, but usually more; *El Fuego Nuevo* requires a battery of thirteen players. Chávez was informative in describing new and exotic instruments and how they were to be played, and he suggested substitutes for instruments that might be difficult to come by. Tunings and special techniques were likewise precisely explained. Inclusion of percussion instruments indigenous to Mexico prevails in those works which were intentionally nationalistic; these native instruments turn up modestly in most of the orchestral works. Use of the piano as a percussion instrument in orchestral works since 1954 is a rather late capitulation to an already well-established contemporary practice. Soli passages for percussion and for percussion with other solo instruments are a consistent syntax of the composer's orchestral language. Passages like the cymbal soli for four players in *Resonancias* bespeak the greatest ingenuity.

Many if not most of the stylistic traits mentioned are the common practice of twentieth-century musical composition. The question then arises, what makes Chávez's music original or different from that of his contemporaries? Part of the answer may be that, because he was largely self-taught in composition, his work does not fall into molds. For that reason, each work has an identity of its own overriding the thread of style which runs through his total output. Another part of the answer can be that there are some unique and tangible features that form a common bond of style. These would have to include Mexican rhythms and melodic figures which though often used in the most subtle way, permeate most of his music. Another is his own brand of dissonance which reveals the singularity of his voice, and finally, what Virgil Thomson has referred to as Chávez's "bumpy counterpoint."[6]

Assessment

The almost universal acclaim Chávez has received and the frequent citation of him as part of a Latin American triumvirate that includes Villa-Lobos and Ginastera has not gone unchallenged, especially in Mexico. There his primacy is rivalled by his contemporary Silvestre Revueltas (1898–1940). Chávez brought Revueltas back to Mexico from the United States in 1929; he placed him as his assistant conductor with the Symphony Orchestra of Mexico, and installed him (in 1934) to teach in the National Conservatory. Chávez encouraged Revueltas to compose and premiered a number of his works with the Mexican orchestra. The compositional style that developed was fresh and natural, reflecting modern-day Mexican nationalism and Revueltas's own Romantic spirit. His music stands out sharply against the more ordered and cerebral output of his mentor, and it was the spontaneity and uninhibited Mexicanism of his work which evoked such an enthusiastic response from the musical public. What began as an amiable association between the two men gradually eroded, ending their professional collaboration.[7]

Chávez took issue with Nicolas Slonimsky's evaluation of him in the *Encyclopedia Britannica* as Mexico's foremost composer. His reaction was, "What do you mean by saying that I am the foremost composer of Mexico? Who are the other composers worth mentioning? Revueltas, yes, but he was my pupil; I made him a composer." Slonimsky asked him about his own teacher Ponce, to which Chávez replied, "Manuel Ponce was never my teacher in any proper sense of the word, and he never was a Mexican nationalist in music; he followed European trends." The composer concluded this topic of conversation by saying, "the only Latin American composers of significance are Villa-Lobos and myself."[8]

It is too soon to know how history will judge Chávez's worth as a composer either in Mexico or internationally. Doubtless, his name will figure in a list of those who have made a significant contribution to that large and disparate body of music known as Mexican or American, and he will have to be counted in the census of international leaders and innovators of style in this century.

Chávez the Conductor

Chávez made his first public appearance as a conductor in 1921 in an inaugural concert of his music in his native Mexico City. The Concerts of New Music he started there in 1924 gave him further experience conducting modern chamber music. Without any formal training in this craft, he learned quickly through experience guided by native musicality and intellect. The musicians' union in Mexico City registered confidence in him both as a conductor and as a potential catalyst for its divided factions in naming him musical director of the Mexican Symphony Orchestra (later called the Symphony Orchestra of Mexico) in 1928.

He proved able to marshall a first-rate musical ensemble, to create new audiences such as workers, children, and radio listeners, to rally financial backing, to introduce music and musicians never before heard in Mexico, and to support other Mexican composers and performing artists. He also took symphonic music to the provinces, a first in Mexico. The orchestra afforded him twenty-one years of valuable conducting experience.

Herbert Barrett published a promotional piece for his Mexican client in 1962 entitled *Carlos Chávez Conductor: 1936 to 1962*. The sixteen-page booklet contains excerpts from reviews of the many orchestras Chávez conducted in those years. Naturally, only favorable comments are included, but the critics clearly had no trouble in finding superlatives even though all of the reviews quoted from were not uniformly glowing. Perhaps more significant is what these reviews tell us of the extent of his activity as a guest conductor and the quality of the orchestras he directed in that quarter of a century. In addition to the major orchestras in the United States—New York, Philadelphia, Boston, Los Angeles, San Francisco, St. Louis, Houston, and New Orleans—and, of course, his own Symphony Orchestra of Mexico, he conducted in Germany, Austria, Norway, Canada, Peru, Argentina, Uruguay, Venezuela, Brazil, and Israel. The list of ensembles he led eventually grew to over one hundred, concluding with his final engagement at the Ninth Interamerican Music Festival in Washington, D.C., in 1978.

Conducting Technique

A favorite Chávez axiom was "the conductor must not command but convince."[9] The gentle persuasion implied in this concept does not wholly agree with his approach to orchestral direction as related by some of the musicians who have played for him. The picture that comes through is of a conductor in total control, one who preferred to dictate every nuance and leave nothing to chance. Gilbert Johnson, who played principal trumpet with the Philadelphia Orchestra, remembers Chávez conducting every note of each cadenza in *Scheherazade*.[10] Bassoonist Luciano Magnanini recalls that the maestro was a stickler for tempos, sometimes even setting or checking a tempo with a pocket metronome during concerts.[11] The impression of Paul Christensen, bass trombonist with the 1971 Cabrillo Festival Orchestra, is of a conductor ". . . somewhat aggressive in concept," who concentrated in rehearsals on perfecting the rhythmic ensemble. His thoroughness and finish, in terms of technique, preparation, and musicianship, go virtually unchallenged. What might be viewed by some as overconducting was simply Chávez's way of abiding by a composer's intentions with painstaking fidelity. Stravinsky admired him as "the conductor most honest to the composer he was conducting."[12] Composer Paul Bowles tells the anecdote that, when Aaron Copland presented the score of his *El Salon México* to Koussevitzky, the venerable conductor returned it saying it would be impossible to conduct. Chávez apparently had no trouble when he directed the world premiere of the piece in 1937.[13] Herbert Weinstock summed up his technique succinctly when he wrote that Chávez's conducting was characterized from the first by rhythmic vigor and a fine command of his forces. "He demands and obtains a constant attention that results in clarity and precision."[14]

It is clear that Chávez knew what he wanted from an orchestra and knew how to get it. He prepared thoroughly, analyzing a work and memorizing it in the process. He conducted from memory except when directing his own works, which he said he could not bear to analyze, and he seldom used a baton (García Morillo, 129). His grasp of what goes into the art of conducting is preserved in a series of four lectures presented at the National Conservatory in 1946; they were published under the title "Initiation to Orchestral Direction" in *Nuestra Música* (nos. 4, 5, 6, and 9, 1946–1948).[15] The fifteen topics addressed range from ear training to the knowledge of each instrument, knowing the form, harmony, and counterpoint in a score, study and exercise of the mechanical methods of conducting, training the memory, understanding the psychological aspects, and finally, interpretation. Unfortunately, this extensive treatise is practically unknown outside of Mexico.

Evaluation

Chávez's debut with the New York Philharmonic on February 11, 1937, evinced a shower of praise in the press. Olin Downes's critique was typical: "So far as euphony and technical finish are concerned, the orchestra surpassed any accomplishment since the days of Toscanini."[16] Byron Belt, reporting on a 1969 concert by the Little Orchestra Society of New York wrote, "Neither Ormandy or Stokowski ever secured more sumptuous sound from an orchestra than Chávez did. . . . He is simply a master conductor."[17] The thirty-two years separating these two reviews and the nine years afterward were filled with an activity which, though secondary to Chávez's main enterprise of composing, has left an indelible mark on the musical world.

The orchestras Chávez conducted, from his first season with the Symphony Orchestra of Mexico in 1928 to his final appearance in Washington, D.C., fifty years later, are listed below in alphabetical order with the year(s) in which the engagements took place.

As Musical Director

Symphony Orchestra of Mexico. Mexico City. 1928–48.

Cabrillo Music Festival Orchestra. Aptos. California. 1970–73.

As Guest Conductor

Albuquerque Symphony Orchestra. 1974.

Ambler Festival Orchestra. Philadelphia. 1969.

Aspen Festival Orchestra. 1961.

BBC Orchestra. London. 1966. 1973.

Bell Aire Symphony. Ellenville. New York. 1956.

Bergen Symphony Orchestra. Bergen. Norway. 1962.

Berlin Philharmonic. 1962.

Bonn Symphony Orchestra. 1964.
Boston Philharmonic Orchestra. 1974.
Boston Symphony Orchestra. 1959.
Brazilian Symphony Orchestra, Río de Janeiro, 1962.
Brooklyn Philharmonia. 1936.
California State University Long Beach Symphony. 1974.
CBS Radio Orchestra. 1936.
Cedar Rapids Symphony Orchestra. 1977.
Chicago Symphony Orchestra. 1941. 1959. 1964.
The Cleveland Symphony Orchestra. 1937. 1956. 1977.
Coolidge Festival Orchestra. Washington. D.C.. 1937.
Dartmouth College Orchestra. Hanover. New Hampshire. 1964.
Del City Center Orchestra. 1960.
Goldman Band. New York. 1974.
Grant Park Concert Orchestra. Chicago. 1975.
Havana Philharmonic. 1947.
Houston Symphony Orchestra. 1946. 1963. 1969.
Indiana State University Orchestra. Terre Haute. 1975.
Interamerican Music Festival Orchestra. Washington. D.C.. 1978.
Israel Philharmonic. Tel Aviv. 1962.
Kalamazoo Symphony Orchestra. 1975.
Kansas City Philharmonic Orchestra. 1968. 1976.
Lewis and Clark College Orchestra. Portland. Oregon. 1964.
The Little Symphony Orchestra. New York. 1969.
London Symphony Orchestra. 1973.
Louisiana State University Orchestra. Baton Rouge. 1975.
Los Angeles Chamber Orchestra. 1952. 1953. 1966.
Los Angeles Philharmonic Orchestra. 1937. 1945. 1952. 1955. 1960. 1966.

The Louisville Orchestra. 1953.
Maracaibo Symphony Orchestra. 1975.
Milwaukee Symphony Orchestra. 1967.
Municipal Theater Orchestra. Río de Janeiro. 1963.
National Symphony Orchestra. Washington. D.C.. 1940. 1943. 1971.
National Symphony Orchestra of Argentina. Buenos Aires. 1956. 1974.
National Symphony Orchestra of Brazil. Río de Janeiro. 1962.
National Symphony Orchestra of the Dominican Republic. Santo Domingo. 1970.
National Symphony Orchestra of Mexico. Mexico City, 1951–53, 1955, 1959, 1960, 1962–68, 1970–71.
National Symphony Orchestra of Peru, Lima, 1941.
National Symphony Orchestra of Spain, Madrid, 1967.
NBC Symphony. 1938.
New England Conservatory Orchestra. Boston. 1959.
New Orleans Philharmonic Symphony Orchestra. 1958. 1961.
New York Philharmonic. 1937. 1960.
New York University Chamber Music Players. 1972.
Northern BBC Orchestra. Manchester. England. 1965.
Oakland Symphony Orchestra. 1969.
North German Radio Network Orchestra. Hamburg. 1962.
Oklahoma City Symphony Orchestra. 1974.
Omaha Symphony Orchestra. 1974.
Orchestra of the National Free University of Mexico, Mexico City, 1963–67, 1971, 1974.
The Orchestra of Puerto Rico, San Juan, 1966.
Peabody Conservatory Orchestra, Baltimore, 1975.

The Philadelphia Orchestra, 1936, 1961.
Philharmonic Orchestra of Buenos Aires,
1966.
Pittsburgh Symphony Orchestra, 1937,
1946, 1961.
Portland Symphony Orchestra. 1953.
Rochester Philharmonic. 1970.
Royal Philharmonic Orchestra. London.
1965.
RTV Orchestra of Belgium. Brussels. 1975.
RTV Orchestra of Spain. Madrid, 1968.
San Antonio Symphony. 1944.
San Diego Symphony Orchestra. 1966.
San Francisco Symphony. 1940. 1944.
San Jose State University Chamber Players.
1975.
San Jose Symphony Orchestra. 1975.
Scottish BBC Orchestra. Edinburgh. 1966.
Seattle Symphony Orchestra. 1956. 1962.
South German Radio Network Orchestra.
Stuttgart. 1966.
Southwest German Radio Network Or-
chestra. Baden-Baden. 1963. 1965.
Stadium Orchestra. New York City. 1959.
State Orchestra of Buenos Aires. Argentina.
1950.

St. Louis Symphony Orchestra. 1939.
1940.
Symphony of the Air. Long Island. New
York. 1963.
Symphony of the BRT. Brussels. 1962.
Symphony Orchestra of the City of Buenos
Aires, 1957.
Symphony Orchestra of Costa Rica. San
José. 1974.
Symphony Orchestra of Guadalajara.
Mexico. 1960. 1964.
Symphony Orchestra of Paris. 1962.
Symphony Orchestra of SODRE,
Montevideo, Uruguay, 1957.
Symphony Orchestra of the University of
San Juan, Argentina, 1974.
Syracuse University Orchestra, Syracuse,
New York, 1976, 1978.
Tucson Symphony Orchestra, 1960.
University of Miami Orchestra, 1955.
Vancouver Symphony Orchestra, 1960.
Venezuelan National Youth Orchestra,
1975, 1976, 1977.
Venezuelan Symphony Orchestra,
Caracas, 1953, 1957.
Vienna Symphony. 1962.

Chávez the Organizer

Chávez was an irrepressible organizer. Mari Carmen Mata said that he could
come into a social gathering and gently but convincingly rearrange the seating of
guests to his liking and theirs.[18] His talent for organization blossomed early. In
1916, when he and his friends put together the literary journal *Gladios*, he was
the one who followed through to obtain a government charter for its publication.
Another pioneering organizational effort was the setting up of Concerts of New
Music in Mexico City during the mid-1920s through which he introduced
Mexican audiences to contemporary chamber music. Virgil Thomson's assessment that he was a man "who made things happen" is applicable again and
again.[19] He had vision, could sustain effort, and could delegate authority to the
right people. A natural analyst, he could quickly dissect a problem and sort out its
components in rational order.[20] He was also a skillful politician; seeing an
opportunity that intrigued him, he would pursue it with all of the influence he

could get to support him, and he usually succeeded.[21] He applied his talent for organization with uncommon drive and an enormous capacity for work, and it affected everything he undertook as a composer, conductor, administrator, teacher, author, lecturer, and as a man.

As Administrator

In revitalizing the National Conservatory in the late 1920s and early 1930s, Chávez restructured the curriculum and faculty and totally redesigned the program of composition instruction. He instituted the Academy of Investigation in the Conservatory to probe Mexico's musical past and to make the results known to musicians and students. When he left the conservatory in 1933, he enlarged the work begun in the Academy of Investigation to include dance and art, and to extend it into the public schools. When incoming President Miguel Alemán decided to create a National Institute of Fine Arts within the Secretariat of Public Education, Chávez was the logical choice to become its director. Not only did he have appropriate background for the job from his experience in the Department of Fine Arts, but he had charisma to add to Alemán's regime. Under Chávez's leadership and massive authority, and backed with an expansive budget, concert life, theater, opera, ballet, and the plastic arts reached unprecedented heights in Mexico.

Chávez left the institute in 1952 to return to composing and conducting, but he was twice more called upon by presidents to reanimate Mexican musical life. At President Adolfo López Mateos's request, he organized, in 1960, a special composition workshop in the National Conservatory for the country's most promising composition talent. His departure coincided with the next change of government in 1964. Luis Echeverría, president from 1970 until 1976, charged Chávez with the task of developing a "national plan" with the goal of bolstering a sagging musical life in Mexico; however the plan never became operational, thus ending Chávez's administrative career in Mexico.

As Teacher

Chávez came from a family of teachers. As early as 1915 (at age sixteen) he was employed as a "professor" by the Secretariat of Public Education. In the two extended periods in which he taught in the National Conservatory (1928–33 and 1960–64), he came into direct teacher-pupil contact with only a few composition students. This situation may have been due, during the earlier period, to the extent of his other activities, but in both periods, only highly qualified and carefully screened students were allowed to matriculate. The earlier composition class consisted of only a handful of members, all of whom later succeeded as prominent music professionals. Chávez trained them thoroughly and opened doors for them in the professional musical establishment. Sandi, Galindo, Contreras, Moncayo, Revueltas *et al.* have contributed measurably to the improvement of music and musical life in Mexico. The Composition Workshop of the early 1960s was even smaller. Of the five (of the original seven) who remained in the program and who chose to follow careers in music, four—Mata, Quintanar, Hernández Medrano, and Villaseñor—all found excellent positions in Mexico, and Mata's conducting career has risen to international proportions.

As Writer

Being in the limelight of Mexican public life, Chávez took advantage of the opportunities available to him to express his views in the press. He contributed to more than a dozen daily newspapers and periodicals in Mexico City, and wrote more than 200 articles for the daily *El Universal* alone beginning as early as 1924.[22] Parts of his book *Toward a New Music* (1937) appeared first as a series of articles in *El Universal* in 1932. He supplied numerous program notes in the early years of the Symphony Orchestra of Mexico and wrote reports on the orchestra's progress and future projections as well as commentaries on his works for program notes of orchestras he guest conducted and liner notes for his own recorded music.

Many of his writings, and obviously those appearing in daily newspapers, were intended for general readership. Aimed at a more specialized and informed reader were his articles for music journals. He himself had a hand in establishing two music journals in Mexico: *Música, Revista Mexicana* in 1930, and *Nuestra Música* in 1946. He contributed to them as well as to United States' periodicals like the *Musical Quarterly* and *Modern Music*. While he wrote on a wide variety of topics, from aesthetics to ethnic music, from avant garde music to jazz, much of his literary energy was directed toward reporting on the musical climate in Mexico, and especially the efforts, successes, and failings of the musical institutions in his country. But whether writing for the generalist or specialist his message was clear, authoritative, and spontaneous. At times he could be caustic in his point of view, but always with humor. Just as in composing he relied mainly on instinct shaped by experience, his literary and journalistic writings depend more on personal feelings and reactions than on scientific investigation.

As Lecturer

Chávez's extensive lecturing began in 1943, the year of his induction into El Colegio Nacional (National College). From that year through 1976 he presented 125 public lectures or lecture concerts sponsored by the National College.[23] Membership in Mexico's Academy of Arts (from 1966) also afforded him opportunities for formal lectures. In 1958, the University of Buffalo invited Chávez to give a series of lectures for one semester. In the same year he accepted the coveted Charles Eliot Norton Poetic Chair at Harvard University. The six Harvard lectures, for which he was paid $3,500 each, were published in 1961 as *Musical Thought.* In his short-term visits to university campuses in the United States in the early 1970s, the focus of attention was mainly on his own music. But wherever he lectured, and on whatever topic, he was direct, in command of his ideas, and in the words of Blas Galindo, "was always able to convince the listener of his point of view."[24]

Chávez the Man

There was a saying in Mexico that "the only dependable things in the country are the 4:00 P.M. Sunday bull fights and Chávez's 9:00 P.M. orchestra downbeat.[25] His meticulous attention to detail saw to an elaborate thirty-point publication checklist, the numbering of each measure in his manuscripts, the placement of an accidental on each note in a chromatic work, and the conducting of every note and nuance in a cadenza. If the definition of a genius as a person "with an infinite capacity for taking pains" is valid, Chávez was at least a strong candidate.

In appearance he was tall, with rugged features and heavy brows that gave him a rather stern countenance. Paul Bowles wrote that "if one had not known he was a composer, one might have taken him for a doctor or lawyer."[26] Normand Lockwood has commented on his "quiet though enormously vital manner."[27] Luis Sandi reports that when Chávez took over the Symphony Orchestra of Mexico in 1928, he had already been seduced by "buen amistad" ("good friendship"), "buen vino" ("good wine"), and "buen amor" ("good love"), but adds that he quickly turned himself into a "work machine."[28] His friend and colleague Virgil Thomson perceived him as "a very dignified, handsome, and proper gentleman." Of Chávez's alleged amorous encounters, Thomson said, "in typical Latin fashion, there was never any public scandal."[29]

Mari Carmen Mata remembers a lighter side to his personality: that of "bon vivant, raconteur, gourmet, and lover of beautiful women."[30] Chávez once wrote that he did not have time to go to parties, but there are reports to the contrary. For example, Herbert Barrett tells of the composer's moving within the most elite social circles in New York, dining and attending parties with the Henry Luces, the William Paleys, and the Nelson Rockefellers. He loved jazz music and would often (in the earlier years) frequent jazz establishments in Harlem with his friend Colin McPhee. He also collected jazz piano records, especially Art Tatum.[31] Once in the late 1960s he went on a special shopping trip and returned with "a stack of Beatles recordings." He wanted to find out what it was in their music that had such universal popular appeal. His conclusion: "they write good melodies."[32]

Chávez was very demanding of quality from those who worked for him but very generous.[33] His New York secretary, Olga Morales, looked forward to going in to work for him; she said he was so warm and considerate, "it was more like a visit with a friend."[34] The comments about the human side of Chávez's personality trace the profile of a discriminating, stable, balanced, and reasonable man who treated the people with whom he came into contact with dignity, respect, and consideration. But his detractors saw him as a musical dictator. He was called the "godfather" of Mexican musical life during the 1973 National Symphony Orchestra dispute. Higinio Velásquez made the outrageous allegation in the press at that time that he was an "inept musician" who had not done anything [for music] in thirty years.[35] Fortunately, he was able to withstand criticism nobly and discreetly. In Henryk Szeryng's words, "He had great authority, ignoring his enemies and being extremely kind to his friends."[36]

Chávez always seemed to have boundless energy. Even at his last conducting engagement in Washington, D.C., in 1978, and while very ill, he managed to get through an almost impossible schedule on the day of the concert. There was a two-hour rehearsal, a reception for him at the Mexican Embassy at 5:00 P.M., the concert at 8:30, and a formal dinner at 10:30. Such was the constitution of Carlos Chávez.

Honors and Awards

Mexico bestowed a number of high honors on its illustrious native in addition to charter membership in the National College (1943) and the Academy of Arts (1966). These awards and distinctions include the National Prize of Arts and Sciences (1958); Gold Medal for Artistic Merit, Chihuahua (1973); Founding Member of the Cultural Center, Córdoba, Veracruz (1976); and the Medal of Merit awarded by the Mexican Institute of Mass Communication (1976).

Honorary recognition from outside of Mexico began in 1932 when he was named Knight of the French Legion of Honor. Belgium honored him in 1950 with the title of Commander of the Order of the Crown, and in 1952 he received three special citations: Commander of the Order of the Polar Star (Switzerland); Official of the French Legion of Honor; and Star of Italian Solidarity. He was awarded Venezuela's *Caro Boesi* Prize in 1954 and was elected to membership in the American Academy of Arts and Sciences and the American Academy of Arts and Letters in 1959 and 1960 respectively. He was named Honorary President of the International Conference on Music and Communication in 1975, and in the same year his name was added to the roster of the *Andrés*

Bello Order in Venezuela. In 1976 he was chosen as an Honorary Fellow of the Costa Rican Musical Union, and the Order of Francisco de Miranda of Venezuela honored him as an inductee the following year. The final award he accepted personally came in the form of an honorary Doctor of Arts degree from Columbia College in Chicago on June 2, 1978.

Fine

Chávez opened new vistas for music and art in Mexico and brought them to a vital realization. His titanic achievement will remain as a bench mark for those who follow him, for the next bearer of Orpheus' lyre. His music stands as a living monument to a formidable creator in the world of contemporary music.

Notes and References

1

1. Among his distinguished ancestors were maternal grandfather Manuel Ramírez Aparicio, a lawyer and poet from Durango, and paternal grandfather José María Chávez who had been governor of the state of Aguascalientes.

2. Roberto García Morillo, *Carlos Chávez: Vida y Obra* (Mexico City and Buenos Aires, 1960), p. 11. In a 1936 interview for the *New York Times* (January 26), Chávez said he looked on "his Indian blood as an invaluable heritage," but he took issue with Nicolas Slonimsky's describing him in print in 1945 as "of partly Indian extraction." Nicolas Slonimsky, in a letter to the present writer, February 14, 1980.

3. Anita Chávez (daughter of the composer), in a conversation with the present writer, August 12, 1980. The three sisters were Nestora, Estefanía, and Ísabel. Carlos's two brothers entered public life in Mexico: Manuel, a lawyer, was his country's ambassador to Holland in the 1950s, and Eduardo became Secretary of Hydraulic Resources.

4. Vivien Perlis, director and interviewer, "Interview with Carlos Chávez," in *Yale School of Music, Oral History Project-American Music Series*, December, 1977.

5. Ibid.

6. This periodical was founded by Chávez and a few of his literary friends including poet Carlos Pellicer. It was suspended after only two issues due to dissension within the group. Carlos Chávez, *Mis Amigos Poetas* (Mexico City, 1977), p. 25.

7. William Weber Johnson, *Heroic Mexico* (Garden City, N.Y., 1968), pp. 272–368.

8. Chávez, *Musical Thought* (Cambridge, Mass., 1961), p. 25.

9. Robert Stevenson, *Music in Mexico* (New York, 1952), p. 239.

10. Chávez, *Falla en México* (Mexico City, 1970), p. 13.

11. Anita Chávez, conversation, August 12, 1980.

12. Anita Chávez, conversation, August 20, 1980.

13. Aaron Copland, *The New Music, 1900–1960* (New York, 1968), p. 147.

14. Paul Rosenfeld, *By Way of Art* (New York, 1928), p. 276.

15. Nicolas Slonimsky, *Music of Latin America* (New York, 1945), p. 232.

16. Stevenson, *Music in Mexico*, p. 239.

17. Betty Kirk, "Ten Years of the Mexico Symphony Orchestra," *New York Times*, October 9, 1938.

18. Stevenson, *Music in Mexico*, pp. 240–41.

19. José Antonio Alcaraz, "La excepción triumfante," *Carlos Chávez: Homenaje Nacional* (Mexico City, 1978), pp. 96–102. This situation mirrors Chávez's rather lukewarm attitude toward Viennese serialism, as does his almost total exclusion of the technique in his own music.

20. Herbert Weinstock, "Carlos Chávez," *Composers of the Americas* (Washington, D.C., 1957), 3:70.

21. Among the more renowned guest conductors were Ansermet, Beecham, Copland, Goosens, Hindemith, Klemperer, Milhaud, Mitropoulis, Monteux, Stokowski, Stravinsky, and Wallenstein. Soloists included Arrau, Casadesus, Copland, Francescatti, List, Ponce, Puig, Revueltas, Sandor, Stern, Szeryng, and many others.

22. Antonio Castro Leal, in a letter to this writer, September 9, 1980.

23. Luis Sandi, "Chávez y la música en México," *Homenaje Nacional*, p. 82.

24. Chávez, "Revolt in Mexico," *Modern Music* 13, no. 3 (March-April, 1936):38.

25. Ibid., p. 39.

26. Chávez, *Musical Thought*, p. 97.

27. Weinstock, "Carlos Chávez," p. 68.

28. Carolina Amor Fornier, in an interview with the present writer, August 8, 1980.

29. Weinstock, "Carlos Chávez," p. 61.

30. Elliott Carter, "Forecast and Review, Late Winter, New York, 1937," *Modern Music* 14, no. 3 (March-April, 1937):151.

31. Chávez, "The Two Persons," *Musical Quarterly* 15, no. 2 (April, 1929):153–59.

32. Chávez, *Toward a New Music* (New York, 1937), p. 8.

33. Herbert Barrett, in an interview with the present writer, November 2, 1979.

34. Stevenson, *Music in Mexico*, p. 243.

35. Howard Shanet, *Philharmonic: A History of New York's Orchestra* (New York, 1975), p. 286.

36. Nicolas Slonimsky, *Music Since 1900* (New York, 1938), p. 424.

37. Weinstock, "Carlos Chávez," p. 61.

38. Colin McPhee, "Scores and Records," *Modern Music* 20, no. 1 (November-December, 1942):51–52.

39. Otto Mayer-Serra, *The Present State of Music in Mexico* (Washington, D.C., 1960), p. 41.

40. John Cage, in a letter to the present writer, April 4, 1980.

41. María Teresa Rodríguez, in a conversation with the present writer, July 24, 1980.

42. "Editorial," *Nuestra Música* 1, no. 1 (March, 1946).

43. Wayne Shirley, comp., *Modern Music 1924–1946, an Analytic Index*, ed. William and Carolyn Lichtenwanger (New York, 1976).

44. "Decreto" [Decree] of the National Institute of Fine Arts, Mexico City, December 31, 1946.

45. Luis Sandi, "Cinquenta Años de Música," *Nuestra Música* 6, no. 23 (1951):228.

46. Mauricio Magdalena, quoted in García Morillo, *Carlos Chávez*, p. 133.

47. Chávez, "Carta a Antonio Rodríguez," *Nuestra Música* 3, no. 10 (April, 1948):102.

48. Jesús Bal y Gay, "El Nacionalismo y la Música Mexicana de Hoy," *Nuestra Música* 4, no. 14 (April, 1949):153.

49. Chávez, "La Sinfónica Nacional," *Nuestra Música* 5, no. 18 (1950):118.

50. Sandi, "Chávez y la Música Mexicana," p. 88.

51. News release among the Chávez documents in *El Centro Nacional de Investigación, Documentación, y Información Musical Carlos Chávez* [The Carlos Chávez National Center for Musical Research, Documentation, and Information], at Calle Liverpool 16, Mexico City.

52. Virgil Thomson, in an interview with the present writer, March 21, 1980.

53. Julián Orbón, conversation, May 5, 1979.

54. Edward Miller, in a letter to the present writer, June 3, 1980.

55. Chávez, *Musical Thought,* p. 116.

56. Slonimsky, letter, April 14, 1980.

57. His music was already well known in Israel. José Serebrier introduced both *Sinfonía Índia* and *Sinfonía de Antígona* in Jerusalem in 1958. The program was taped and played widely throughout the country. José Serebrier, in a letter to the present writer, August 2, 1980.

58. *Carlos Chávez Press,* 1966–1974 (New York: Herbert Barrett, n.d.).

59. Orbón, conversation, May 5, 1979.

60. Rodríguez, conversation, July 24, 1980.

61. Humberto Hernández Medrano, in a conversation with the present writer, August 6, 1980.

62. Ibid.

63. The studio mixing of the album was done by Eduardo Mata. Mata, inverview, August 13, 1980.

64. Published in a revised form but with the same basic message: *Lira de Orfeo* (Mexico City: Editorial de El Colegio Nacional, 1972).

65. *Excelsior,* January 18, 1973.

66. *Excelsior,* April 30, 1972.

67. *The News,* January 4, 1973.

68. *Diario de la Tarde,* January 4, 1973.

69. Mata, interview, August 13, 1980.

70. *Excelsior,* January 23, 1973.

71. Ibid.

72. *San Jose Mercury News,* April 12, 1970.

73. Carl Christensen, a member of the 1971 festival orchestra, in a letter to this writer, August 27, 1980.

74. Olga Morales, in a conversation with the present writer, October 30, 1980.

75. Miguel Coelho, interview, October 23, 1980.

76. Arthur Cohn, interview, October 24, 1980.

77. Serebrier, letter, August 2, 1980.

78. Reported by María Teresa Rodríguez, wife of Dr. de la Sierra, in a conversation with the present writer, August 11, 1980.

2

1. Cecil Michener Smith, "Forecast and Review," *Modern Music* 14, no. 3 (March-April, 1936):114.

2. Vivien Perlis, "Interview," p. 3.

3. Ibid.

4. Aaron Copland, *The New Music,* p. 147.

5. Robert Floyd, in a conversation with this writer, January 24, 1982.

6. Copland, *The New Music,* p. 148.

7. Aaron Copland, "Scores and Records," *Modern Music* 14, no. 3 (March-April, 1936):99.

8. *Cabrillo Music Festival Program,* 1971.

9. Chávez, *Musical Thought,* pp. 53–84.

10. William Masselos, in a conversation with the present writer, November 4, 1980.

11. Quoted in the preface of *Estudio a Rubinstein* (New York: G. Schirmer, Inc., 1976).

12. Alan Marks, record liner notes for *American Contemporary.* CRI SD 385.

13. Masselos, conversation, November 4, 1980.

3

1. Herbert Weinstock, "Chávez Lights a New Fire," *United Nations World Magazine* 4, no. 6 (June, 1950):58.

2. Nicolas Slonimsky, *Music Since 1900*, p. 336.

3. Marc Blitzstein, "Forecast and Review," *Modern Music* 9, no. 3 (March-April, 1932):124.

4. Odyssey Y 31534.

5. *Mexican Music: Notes by Herbert Weinstock for Concerts Arranged by Carlos Chávez* (New York, 1940), pp. 5–13.

6. Preface to *Xochipilli, an Imagined Aztec Music* (New York: Mills Music, Inc., 1964).

7. Preface to *Tambuco* (New York: Mills Music, Inc., 1967).

8. Gerard Béhague, *Music in Latin America: An Introduction* (Englewood Cliffs, N.J., 1979), p. 290, Joan Sweeney Coombs, "Carlos Chávez: A Reassessment of His Place in Twentieth-Century Music" (Master's thesis, University of Alabama, 1981), pp. 64–65. Coombs also points out some minimal twelve-tone treatment at the beginning of the Preludio.

4

1. Chávez, *Mis Amigos Poetas* (Mexico City, 1977), pp. 12–26.

2. Colin McPhee, "Scores and Records," *Modern Music* 20, no. 2 (January-February, 1943):128.

3. Quoted in García Morillo, p. 104.

4. Virgil Thomson, interview, March 21, 1980.

5. Donald Fuller, "Forecast and Review," *Modern Music* 19, no. 4 (May-June, 1942):257.

6. Chávez, *Mis Amigos Poetas*, pp. 12–26.

5

1. A seventh symphony, listed in Rodolfo Halffter's catalog as having been commissioned by Lea Brants de Falcón was never written; there is no such composition as the orchestral suite *Fuego Olímpico* cited in *The Dictionary of Composers and their Music* (New York, 1978), p. 63.

2. Jesús Bal y Gay, "La 'Sinfonía de Antígona' de Carlos Chávez," *Nuestra Música* 5, no. 17 (1st Trimester, 1950):14.

3. Miguel Coelho, in a conversation with this writer, October 23, 1980.

4. María Teresa Rodríguez reports that when she first met Chávez in 1952, he appeared to have a jaundiced condition and said he was treating it with a folk remedy. Rodríguez, conversation, August 11, 1980.

5. Aaron Copland, "Festival of Contemporary Latinamerican Music," *Tempo* (Spring, 1955), p. 5.

6. Franz Reinzenstein, "The International Society of Contemporary Music at Baden-Baden," *Tempo* 36 (Summer, 1955):8.

7. Aaron Copland, *The New Music*, p. 150.

8. *Notas a 8 Obras de Carlos Chávez* (Mexico City, 1964), p. 5.

9. Gloria Carmona, program notes for *Symphony VI* in *Concierto Sinfónico*, September 13, 1970 (Mexico City: Academia de Artes, 1979), pp. 6–7.

10. *Notas a 8 Obras de Carlos Chávez*, pp. 5–6.

11. Ibid, p. 6.

12. Alfred Frankenstein, "Forecast and Review," *Modern Music* 22, no. 4 (May-June, 1945):264.

13. Aaron Copland, *The New Music*, pp. 148–49.

14. Otto Mayer-Serra, *The Present State of Music in Mexico*, p. 41.

15. Gerard Béhague, *Music in Latin America*, pp. 138–39.

16. CBS 32 11 0064.

17. Szeryng reports that he had worked closely with the composer in revising the *Concerto* since 1961, shortening the cadenza and rendering certain passages more idiomatic for the violin. Szeryng, in a letter, December 26, 1980.

18. Coelho, conversation, October 23, 1980.

19. Nicolas Slonimsky, *Music Since 1900*, p. 932.

20. Per Brevig, in an interview with this writer, October 26, 1980.

6

1. Arthur Cohn, in an interview with this writer October 24, 1980. The fuller orchestration calls for 2 piccolos, 2 flutes, 2 oboes, English horn, Eb clarinet, 2 Bb clarinets, bass clarinet, 3 bassoons, 4 horns, 4 trumpets, 3 trombones, tuba, timpani, and strings. The small version is for 2 flutes, oboe, clarinet, 2 bassoons, 2 horns, 2 trumpets, 2 trombones, and strings.

2. Program of the 1970 Cabrillo Music Festival.

3. *Sämtliche Orgelwerke* (Wiesbaden: Breitkopf und Härtel, 1971, 1972), vol. 1, part 2, p. 129.

4. Colin McPhee, "Scores and Records," *Modern Music* 17, no. 1 (October-November, 1939):52.

5. *Antonio Vivaldi* (Milan: Edizione Ricordi, 1966), vol. 436.

6. Alfred Frankenstein, "Forecast and Review," *Modern Music* 21, no. 3 (April-May, 1944):174.

7. Slonimsky, *Music in Latin America*, p. 233.

8. Cohn, interview.

9. Quoted by William Flanagan in the notes to the recording *Music of Mexico* (Decca DL 9527).

10. Gilbert Chase, *A Guide to the Music of Latin America* (Washington, D.C., 1962), p. 270.

11. Miguel Coelho, conversation, November 7, 1980.

12. Cohn, interview.

13. In the preface to the score, Chávez reports that the refurbishing of the earlier *Llamadas* took place in 1967 as opposed to the 1973 date indicated in the official update of the catalog of works.

14. Preface to *Mañanas Mexicanas* (New York: Carl Fischer, Inc., 1977).

15. David Ewen, *The World of Twentieth-Century Music* (Englewood Cliffs, N.J., 1968), p. 160.
16. Slonimsky, *Music Since 1900*, 4th edition, p. 1178.
17. Byron Belt, *Long Island Press*, March 12, 1969.
18. Program of the 1970 Cabrillo Music Festival.
19. Farley Hutchins, program notes for the Akron Symphony Orchestra, October 9, 1973.

7

1. Chávez, notes to the recording *Carlos Chávez* (Columbia M 32685).
2. Slonimsky, *Music in Latin America*, p. 215.
3. Weinstock, *Mexican Music*, p. 26.
4. Marc Blitzstein, "Forecast and Review," *Modern Music* 9, no. 4 (May-June, 1932):166.
5. Mata, interview, August 13, 1980.
6. Tom Null, notes to the recording *Bernstein Conducts Bernstein, Chávez Conducts Chávez* (Varese/Sarabande 81055).
7. Plot described by Anna Kisselgoff in "Dance: Martha Graham's Troupe in 'Dark Meadow,'" *New York Times*, May 29, 1977.
8. Jesús Bal y Gay, "La Hija de Cólquide de Carlos Chávez," *Nuestra Música* 5, no. 19 (3rd Trimester, 1950):212.
9. Chávez, notes to the recording *Carlos Chávez* (Columbia M 32685).
10. The tape, as well as the manuscripts of *Pirámide*, are in the custody of Miguel Coelho, the composer's former assistant in New York.
11. Coelho, conversation, October 23, 1980.
12. An arrangement of *Tierra Mojada* for chorus and orchestra is listed as having been performed in 1943 by the Symphony Orchestra of Mexico in its repertory list. The arrangement is not included in the catalog of works, and it does not appear in the inventory of his manuscripts in the Performing Arts Library at Lincoln Center in New York.
13. Weinstock, "Carlos Chávez," p. 69.
14. Weinstock, *Mexican Music*, p. 23.
15. Program of the 1972 Cabrillo Music Festival.
16. A tape recording of this performance was made available to the present writer through the courtesy of Tonatiuh de la Sierra Rodríguez.
17. The production was made possible with help from Kirstein and the Alice M. Ditson Fund of the Department of Music, Columbia University.
18. Noel Lindsay, review in the *Christian Science Monitor*, November 7, 1959.
19. A tape recording of this performance was made available by Miguel Coelho.
20. Cohn, interview, October 24, 1980.

8

1. *Chávez: Homenaje Nacional*, p. 17.
2. He travelled on a Mexican diplomatic passport. Arthur Cohn, interview, October 24, 1980.
3. Antonio Castro Leal, letter, September 9, 1980.
4. *Chávez: Homenaje Nacional*, p. 17.

5. Miguel Coelho, interview, October 23, 1980.

6. Virgil Thomson, interview, March 21, 1980.

7. Chávez did not program any of Revueltas's music after 1935 until the latter's death in 1940. He campaigned actively for the assignment to write the score for the Mexican film classic *Redes* (1935) but lost out to Revueltas. Castro Leal, letter, September 9, 1980. The only "media" music Chávez wrote was a group of television commercials for Channel 13 in Mexico City. He included one of these, *Tema Equis* [Theme Ten]. in his catalog of works.

8. Nicolas Slonimsky, letter, February 14, 1980.

9. Newlon, *The Men Who Made Mexico*, p. 216.

10. Gilbert Johnson, in a conversation with the present writer, September 6, 1980.

11. Luciano Magnanini, in a conversation with this writer, September 5, 1980.

12. Laura Villaseñor, in an interview with this writer, August 1, 1980.

13. Paul Bowles, in a letter to the present writer, July 19, 1980.

14. Weinstock, "Carlos Chávez," p. 71.

15. Later issued as a single book in Mexico.

16. Quoted in Stevenson, *Music in Mexico*, p. 243.

17. *Long Island Press*, March 12, 1979.

18. Mari Carmen Mata, in an interview with this writer, August 13, 1980.

19. Thomson, interview, March 21, 1980.

20. Hernández Medrano, interview, August 6, 1980.

21. Castro Leal, letter, September 9, 1980.

22. For a listing of these articles to 1960, see García Morillo, pp. 230–37.

23. A complete list of Chávez's National College lectures is available through El Colegio Nacional, Calle de Luis González Obregón No. 23, México 1, D.F.

24. Galindo, interview, August 25, 1980.

25. Manuel de la Cera Alonso, in an interview with this writer, August 13, 1980.

26. Bowles, letter, July 19, 1980.

27. Normand Lockwood, in a letter to this writer, May 23, 1980.

28. Luis Sandi, "Cinquenta Años de Música en México," *Nuestra Música* 6, no. 23 (3rd Trimester, 1951):228.

29. Thomson, interview, March 21, 1980.

30. Mari Carmen Mata, interview, August 13, 1980.

31. Herbert Barrett, interview, November 2, 1979.

32. M.C. Mata, interview, August 13, 1980.

33. Coelho, interview, October 23, 1980.

34. Morales, conversation, October 30, 1980.

35. *Excelsior*, March 23, 1973.

36. Szeryng, letter, December 26, 1980.

Catalog of Musical Works

Chávez's musical output has been cataloged in four publications to date. The first two were issued by the Pan American Union: *Carlos Chávez, Catalog of his Works*, Music Series 10 (Washington, 1944); and *Composers of the Americas*, 3 (Washington, 1957); 60–82. The third is appended to García Morillo's 1960 biography of the composer; it includes compositions written before 1959. The Society of Authors and Composers of Mexico undertook the publication of a catalog which appeared in 1971. This *Catalogo Completo de sus Obras* [Complete Catalog of his Works], prepared by Rodolfo Halffter in collaboration with Carmen Sordo Sodi and Alicia Muñiz Hernández, includes works written as late as 1968. The present update of the aforementioned catalogs was made possible with information supplied by Sra. Anita Chávez and by inspection of the composer's manuscripts in the Library of the Performing Arts, Lincoln Center, New York City.

In the present catalog, date of composition appears to the left of the title; place of publication, and publication date follow the title. Works available only on rental from the publisher do not show a publication date. Absence of place, publisher, and date indicates that the composition is still in manuscript. Not included in this catalog are some early works the composer either destroyed or chose to exclude from the official catalogs. The early works he preserved may have been those he held in higher esteem, or perhaps he saw in them some foreshadowing of directions his music would take in later years. His own statement on this point leaves room for both interpretations. "Many of these compositions I destroyed, others no—some because they may be of some documentary value, others because they may be of some incipient worth." (Halffter, Foreword.) Among the extant early works not listed in the catalogs are some dozen or so student compositions, mostly for piano, or violin and piano, written between 1911 and 1918. They are among those manuscripts on deposit at the Library of the Performing Arts at Lincoln Center. They are not included in the following chronology.

1915   *Adelita y la Cucaracha*, arranged for solo piano. Mexico City: A. Wagner y Levien Sucs., 1920.
        Sinfonía para Orquesta.

1917   *Preludio y Fuga* for solo piano.

1918   *Anda buscando de rosa en rosa* for solo piano. Mexico City: A. Wagner y Levien Sucs., 1920.
        Berceuse for solo piano. Mexico City: A. Wagner y Levien Sucs., 1920.
        Carnaval, Twenty pieces on ASCH for solo piano.
        Esperanza Ingenua for solo piano.
        Extase for soprano or tenor and piano, Spanish text after Victor Hugo.
        Extase, reduction for solo piano. Mexico City: A. Wagner y Levien Sucs., 1920.

Gavotte for solo piano.
Meditación for solo piano.
Pensamiento Feliz for solo piano.
Sonata Fantasia [Sonata I] for solo piano.
Triste Sonrisa for solo piano.

1919   *Adiós, adiós* for solo piano.
Barcarola for solo piano.
Deuxième Sonate pour Piano. Berlin: Bote und Bock, 1923.
Du bist wie eine Blume for soprano or tenor and piano, Spanish text after Heinrich Heine.
Estrellas Fijas for soprano or tenor and piano, Text by Asunción Silva.
Estudio I for solo piano.
Estudio II for solo piano.
Las Margaritas arranged for solo piano.
Sexteto de Arcos y Piano for 2 violins, viola, 2 cellos, and piano.
Vals Íntimo I for solo piano.
Vals Íntimo II for solo piano. Mexico City: A. Wagner y Levien Sucs., 1920.

1920   *Bendición* for solo piano. Mexico City: A. Wagner y Levien Sucs., 1920.
Cuando empieza a caer la tarde arranged for solo piano.
Estudio III for solo piano.
Noche, Aguafuerte for solo piano.
Vals Íntimo III for solo piano.
Vals Íntimo IV for solo piano

1921   *Á l'Aube, Image Mexicaine,* arrangement of "Las Mañanitas" for solo piano. Berlin: Bote und Bock, 1923.
Cuarteto de Arcos I for two violins, viola, and cello.
El Fuego Nuevo, Ballet Azteca for SATB chorus and orchestra. Plot by the composer.
El Fuego Nuevo, reduction for unison chorus and piano.
Estudio IV for solo piano.
Madrigals I–V for solo piano.
Vals Elegía for solo piano.

1922   *Cuatro Nocturnos* for solo piano.
Jarabe, arranged for solo piano.
Madrigals VI and VII for solo piano.

1923   *Aspectos I and II* for solo piano.
Imagen Mexicana, traditional song for a cappella chorus.
Inutil Epigrama for soprano or tenor and piano. Spanish text after Ronald de Carvalho.
Polígonos for solo piano. New York: Mills Music, Inc., 1961.
Three Pieces for Guitar. New York: Mills Music, Inc., 1962.
Tres Exágonos for soprano or tenor and piano, Spanish text by Carlos Pellicer.
Tres Exágonos, version for soprano or tenor, flute doubling piccolo, oboe doubling English horn, bassoon, and viola.

1924   *Otros Tres Exágonos* for soprano or tenor, flute, oboe, bassoon, piano, and viola.
        Spanish text by Carlos Pellicer.
        Sonatina for Piano. New York: Boosey & Hawkes, 1930 (originally New York:
        Coscob, 1930).
        Sonatina for Cello and Piano. New York: Mills Music, Inc., 1966.
        Sonatina for Violin and Piano. New York: Mills Music, Inc., 1966 (originally
        San Francisco: New Music, 1928).

1925   *Energía for Nine Instruments* for piccolo, flute, bassoon, horn, trumpet, bass
        trombone, viola, cello, and double bass. New York: Mills Music, Inc., 1968.
        Foxtrot for solo piano.
        Los Cuatro Soles, Ballet Indígena for soprano soloist, optional SA chorus and
        orchestra. Plot by the composer.
        Los Cuatro Soles, Ballet Indígena, version for soprano soloist, SA chorus, and
        small orchestra.
        Los Cuatro Soles, reduction for soprano soloist, optional SA chorus, and piano.
        36 for solo piano. New York: Mills Music, Inc., 1961 (originally San Francisco:
        New Music, 1930).

1926   *Caballos de Vapor, Sinfonía de Baile* for large orchestra. Plot by the composer.
        New York: Boosey & Hawkes.
        Caballos de Vapor, reduction of the ballet, for two pianos. New York: Boosey &
        Hawkes.
        Solo for piano. New York: Mills Music, Inc., 1961.
        Suite from Caballos de Vapor for orchestra. New York: Boosey & Hawkes, 1958.

1928   *Blues* for solo piano. New York: Mills Music, Inc., 1961.
        Fox for solo piano. New York: Mills Music, Inc., 1961.
        Sonata [III] for solo piano. Mexico City: Ediciones Mexicanas de Música, 1972
        (originally San Francisco: New Music, 1933).

1929   *Sonata for Four Horns,* unaccompanied. New York: Mills Music, Inc., 1967.

1930   *Paisaje* for solo piano. New York: Mills Music, Inc., 1961.
        Unidad, part of *Seven Pieces for Piano,* with *Polígonos, 36, Solo, Blues, Fox,*
        and *Paisaje.* New York: Mills Music, Inc., 1961 (originally San Francisco:
        New Music, 1936).

1932   *Antígona, Sketches for the Symphony* for piccolo, flute, oboe, English horn,
        clarinet, trumpet, harp, and two percussionists.
        Cuarteto de Arcos II for violin, viola, cello, and double bass.
        Tierra Mojada/Wet Earth for SATB chorus, oboe, and English horn. Spanish text
        by Ramón López Velarde, English translation by Noel Lindsay. New York:
        Boosey & Hawkes.
        Tierra Mojada arranged for a cappella chorus. New York: Boosey & Hawkes,
        1961.
        Todo/All for mezzo soprano or baritone. Spanish text by Ramón López Velarde,
        English translation by Noel Lindsay. New York: Boosey & Hawkes, 1958
        (published jointly with *North Carolina Blues* as *Dos Canciones*).

1933 *Cantos de Mexico* for Mexican orchestra.
Sinfonía de Antígona for orchestra. New York: G. Schirmer, Inc., 1948.

1934 *El Sol, Corrido Mexicano* for SATB chorus and orchestra. Traditional verses and poems by Carlos Gutiérrez Cruz, English translation by Noel Lindsay. New York: Mills Music, Inc., 1962.
El Sol, Corrido Mexicano, reduction for SATB chorus and piano.
El Sol, Corrido Mexicano, arranged for band and optional SATB chorus. New York: Mills Music, Inc., 1962.
Soli [I] for oboe, clarinet, trumpet, and bassoon. New York: Boosey & Hawkes, 1959.
Llamadas, Sinfonía Proletaria for SATB chorus and orchestra. Verses from the *Ballad of the Mexican Revolution.*
Llamadas, Sinfonía Proletaria, reduction for SATB chorus and piano. Mexico City: Ediciones Palacio de Bellas Artes, 1934.
Three Spirals for violin and piano. New York: Mills Music, Inc., 1969 (Spiral I, San Francisco: New Music, 1935).

1935 *Chapultepec, Three Famous Mexican Pieces* for orchestra; originally entitled *Obertura Republicana.* New York: Mills Music, Inc., 1968.
Chapultepec, Three Famous Mexican Pieces, arranged for band. New York: Mills Music, Inc., 1963.
Sinfonía India for orchestra. New York: G. Schirmer, Inc., 1950. (Band arrangement by Frank Ericson. New York: G. S. Schirmer, Inc., 1971).

1937 *Chaconne in E minor by Buxtehude* for large or small orchestra. New York: Mills Music, Inc., 1962.
Concerto for Four Horns and Orchestra, adapted from *Sonata for Four Horns* (1929). New York: Mills Music, Inc., 1967.
Ten Preludes for Piano. New York: G. Schirmer, Inc., 1940.

1938 *Concerto for Piano with Orchestra.* New York: G. Schirmer, Inc., 1942; revised 1969.
Concerto for Piano with Orchestra, reduction for two pianos. New York: G. Schirmer, Inc., 1942; revised 1969.
Three Poems for Voice and Piano for soprano or tenor. Spanish texts by Carlos Pellicer, Salvador Novo, and Xavier Villaurrutia, English translations by Willis Wager. New York: G. Schirmer, Inc., 1942.

1939 *Four Nocturnes* for soprano and contralto with orchestra. Spanish texts by Xavier Villaurrutia, English translation by Noel Lindsay, and German translation by Rudolf Peyer.
Four Nocturnes, reduction for soprano, contralto, and piano.

1940 *La Paloma Azul/The Blue Dove* for small orchestra and chorus; traditional Mexican song with original text in Spanish and translations into English, French, and German. New York: Boosey & Hawkes, 1956.
La Paloma Azul/The Blue Dove for SATB chorus and piano. New York: Boosey & Hawkes, 1956.
Para Juanita for solo piano.

Trio for flute, harp, and viola; version of four pieces by Debussy and Falla.
Xochipilli, an Imagined Aztec Music for piccolo, flute, Eb clarinet, trombone, and six percussionists. New York: Mills Music, Inc., 1964.

1941   *Himno Nacional Mexicano de Jaime Nunó,* arranged for orchestra.
La Casada Infiel/The Faithless Wife for singer [*canto*] and piano; Spanish text by Federico García Lorca, English translation by Noel Lindsay. Mexico City: Ediciones Mexicanos de Música, 1960 and New York: Southern Music Publishing Co., Inc., 1960.
Sonata IV for Piano.

1942   *A! Freedome* for a cappella chorus; fourteenth-century English text, modern English translation by Willis Wager. New York: G. Schirmer, Inc., 1947.
Fugas para Piano.
Four Traditional Indian Melodies from Ecuador for soprano or tenor, flute, oboe, Eb clarinet, bassoon, violins I and II, viola, cello, double bass, and two percussionists; original Spanish texts.
Miniatura, Homenaje a Carl Deis, fugue for solo piano.
North Carolina Blues for mezzo soprano or baritone and piano. Spanish text by Xavier Villaurrutia, English translation by Noel Lindsay. New York: Boosey & Hawkes, 1958 (published jointly with *Todo* as *Dos Canciones*).
Three Nocturnes for a cappella chorus. New York: G. Schirmer, Inc., 1946.
Toccata for Percussion Instruments for six percussionists. New York: Mills Music, Inc., 1954 (originally Los Angeles: Affiliated Musicians, Inc., 1954).
Tree of Sorrow/Arbolucu, te sequeste, arranged for a cappella chorus; Spanish/English bilingual text of traditional Spanish verses. New York: Music Press, Inc., 1949.
A Woman is a Worthy Thing for a cappella chorus; anonymous fifteenth-century poem. New York: G. Schirmer, Inc., 1947.

1943   *Concerto in G minor, Op. 6, No. 1 of Vivaldi* for orchestra.
Cuarteto de Arcos III for two violins, viola, and cello (movements II, III, and IV of *La Hija de Cólquide*).
Danza de la Pluma, arranged for solo piano.
La Hija de Cólquide for flute, oboe, clarinet, bassoon, and string quartet; plot by Martha Graham, later titled *Dark Meadow.* New York: Mills Music, Inc.
La Hija de Cólquide, reduction for solo piano. New York: Mills Music, Inc.
La Llorona, arranged for solo piano; in Miguel Covarrubias, *The Isthmus of Tehuantepec.* New York: Alfred Knopf Inc., 1946, p. 323.
Saraband for Strings from La Hija de Cólquide, arrangement of No. VII, for string orchestra. New York: Mills Music, Inc., 1966.
Suite for Double Quartet from La Hija de Cólquide for flute, oboe, clarinet, bassoon, and string quartet. New York: Mills Music, Inc., 1967.
Suite Sinfónica de La Hija de Cólquide for orchestra. New York: Mills Music, Inc., 1968 (originally Mexico City: Ediciones Mexicanos de Música, 1951).

1946   *Canto a la Tierra* for unison chorus and piano; text by Enrique Gonzales Martínez. Mexico City: Ediciones Mexicanos de Música, 1946.

1946   *Canto a la Tierra,* version for unison chorus, 2 horns, 2 trumpets, 2 trombones, and tuba.
        Canto a la Tierra, version for unison chorus and orchestra.

1947   *Tocata para Orquesta.* Incidental music for a scene from *Don Quixote de la Mancha.*

1948   *Concerto for Violin and Orchestra.* New York: Mills Music, Inc., 1964.
        Concerto for Violin and Orchestra, reduction for violin and piano. New York: Mills Music, Inc. 1964.

1949   *Estudio IV, Homenaje a Chopin* for solo piano. Mexico City: Ediciones Mexicanos de Música, 1949 and New York: Southern Music Publishing Co., Inc., 1949.
        Three Etudes for Piano, a Chopin. New York: Mills Music, Inc., 1969.

1950   *Left Hand Inversions of Five Chopin Etudes for Piano.* New York: Mills Music, Inc., 1968.

1951   *Happy Birthday* arranged for a cappella chorus.
        Sinfonía No. 3 for orchestra. New York: Boosey & Hawkes, 1955.

1952   *Cuatro Nuevos Estudios para Piano.*

1953   *Baile, Cuadro Sinfónico* for orchestra; originally the third movement of *Symphony No. 4.*
        Sinfonía No. 5 for string orchestra. New York: Mills Music, Inc., 1964.
        Symphony No. 4: Sinfonía Romántica for orchestra; new third movement added October, 1953, see *Baile.* New York: Boosey & Hawkes, 1959.
        The Visitors, an opera in three acts for soprano, contralto, tenor, baritone, and bass soloists, SATB chorus, and orchestra; original libretto in English by Chester Kallman, Spanish translation by Noel Lindsay and Eduardo Hernández Moncada; previous titles were *Panfilo and Lauretta* and *Love Propitiated.*

1953   *The Visitors,* an opera in three acts, reduction for five solo voices and piano.

1956   *Prometheus Bound,* a cantata for soprano, contralto, tenor, baritone, and bass soloists, SATB chorus and orchestra; based on Aeschylus's tragedy.

1957   *Upingos,* a melody for oboe solo.

1958   *Invención [I]* for solo piano. New York: Boosey & Hawkes, 1960.

1960   *Sonata V for Piano;* on a harmonic scheme of Mozart K 533/494.

1961   *Soli No. II for Wind Quintet* for flute, oboe, clarinet, horn, and bassoon. New York: Mills Music, Inc., 1963.
        Sonata VI for Piano. New York: Mills Music, Inc., 1965.
        VI Symphony for Orchestra. New York: Mills Music, Inc., 1965.

1962   *Lamentaciones* for soprano or tenor, piccolo, oboe, marimba, and bass drum; Spanish text translated from Nahuatl by Antonio María Garibay.

1964   *Fuga H A G, C* for violin, viola, cello, and double bass.
        Resonancias for Orchestra. New York: Mills Music, Inc., 1966.
        Tambuco, for Six Percussion Players. New York: Mills Music, Inc., 1967.

1965   *Invention No. 2* for violin, viola, and cello. New York: Mills Music, Inc., 1966.
        Soli No. 3 for bassoon, trumpet, viola, timpani, and orchestra. New York: Mills
        Music, Inc., 1967.

1966   *Soli No. 4* for brass trio (trumpet, horn, and trombone). New York: Boosey &
        Hawkes, 1976.

1967   *Elatio* for orchestra.
        Invention III for Harp. New York: Mills Music, Inc., 1969.
        Mañanas Mexicanas for solo piano after *Llamadas* (1934).

1968   *Fragmento* for a cappella speaking chorus from *Pirámide.* New York: Carl
        Fischer, 1976.
        Pirámide, Ballet in Four Acts for orchestra, SATB chorus, and prepared magnetic
        tape; plot by the composer. *Orchestral Suite.* New York: Carl Fischer, in
        preparation.
        Vocalización Aguda [High Vocalization] for coloratura soprano and piano.

1969   *Clio, Symphonic Ode* for orchestra. New York: G. Schirmer, Inc., 1970.
        Discovery for orchestra. New York: G. Schirmer, Inc., 1971.
        Variations for Violin and Piano. New York: G. Schirmer, Inc., 1971.

1971   *Initium para Orquesta.* New York: Belwin Mills, 1975.

1972   *Nonantsin* for a cappella chorus; traditional Indian melody, Indian text with
        phonetic guide to Spanish and English. New York: Tetra Music Corp.,
        1976.
        Tema Equis, a television theme for chorus and small instrumental ensemble.

1973   *Estudio a Rubinstein* for solo piano. New York: G. Schirmer, Inc., 1976.
        Four Variations for piano from Mañanas Mexicanas. Adapted from Part I of
        Paisajes Mexicanos (1973).
        Paisajes Mexicanos for orchestra. A reworking of *Llamadas* (1934).
        Partita for Solo Timpani. New York: G. Schirmer, Inc., in preparation.

1974   *Epistle To Be Left on the Earth* for a cappella chorus; text by Archibald MacLeish.
        New York: Tetra Music Corp., 1976.
        Feuille D'Album for guitar.
        Nokwik for speaking chorus; Indian text with phonetic guide to English. New
        York: Tetra Music Corp., 1976.
        A Pastoral for a cappella chorus; sixteenth-century text "In the Merry Month of
        May." New York: Tetra Music Corp., 1976.
        Mañanas Mexicanas for symphonic band. Arrangement of the first half of
        Paisajes Mexicanos (1973). New York: Carl Fischer, 1977.
        Rarely, Rarely for a cappella chorus; text by Shelley. New York: Tetra Music
        Corp., 1976.

Sonante for String Orchestra.

Tzintzuntzan for band; arrangement of the second half of *Paisajes Mexicanos* (1973). New York: Carl Fischer, in preparation.

The Waning Moon for a cappella chorus; text by Shelley. New York: Tetra Music Corp., 1976.

1975 *Concerto for Violoncello and Orchestra.* Incomplete.

Five Caprichos for solo piano. New York: G. Schirmer, Inc., in preparation.

Four Variations for piano from Mañanas Mexicanas (1967).

1976 *Zandunga Serenade* for band. New York: Carl Fischer, 1977.

Concerto for Trombone and Orchestra. New York: G. Schirmer, Inc., in preparation.

Concerto for Trombone and Orchestra, reduction for trombone and piano. New York: G. Schirmer, Inc., 1982.

Discography

Caballos de Vapor (Horsepower) Suite

Louisville Symphony Orchestra, Jorgé
    Mester conducting   Louisville 713

"Danza Moderna Mexicana" Orchestra of
    the National Free University of Mexico,
    Eduardo Mata conducting   RCA MKLA–65

Chaconne in E Minor by Buxtehude

National Symphony Orchestra of Mexico,
    Chávez conducting   CBS 32 11 0064

Concerto for Piano with Orchestra

Eugene List and the Vienna State Opera
    Orchestra, Chávez conducting   West. XWN 19030

María Teresa Rodríguez and the New
    Philharmonia Orchestra, Eduardo
    Mata conducting   RCA ARL 1–3341

Concerto for Violin and Orchestra

Henryk Szeryng and the National Symphony
    Orchestra of Mexico, Chávez
    conducting   CBS 32 11 0064

Corrido El Sol

Orchestra and chorus of the National Free
    University of Mexico, Eduardo Mata
    conducting   UNAM VVMN 7

"Music of Mexico" The Symphony
    Orchestra of Mexico, Chávez
    conducting   Decca DL 9527

Danza a Centéotl from *Los Cuatro Soles*

"Carlos Chávez Directs Mexican Music,"
    Mexican Orchestra and chorus   CBS CLS–5369

152

Discovery

    Orchestra of the National Free University of
Mexico, Eduardo Mata conducting   RCA MRS–003

Estudio a Rubinstein

    "American Contemporary," Alan Marks,
piano   CRI SD 385

Five Caprichos

    "American Contemporary," Alan Marks,
piano   CRI SD 385

Invención [Invention]

    María Teresa Rodríguez, piano   UNAM VVMN +

La Hija de Cólquide [The Daughter of Cholchis]
    Suite

    The Symphony Orchestra of Mexico, Chávez
conducting   Decca DL 7512

    The National Symphony Orchestra of
Mexico, Chávez conducting   Varese/Sarabande 81055

La Paloma Azul [The Blue Dove]

    "Carlos Chávez Directs Mexican Music"
Mexican Orchestra and chorus   CBS CLS–5369

Los Cuatro Soles [The Four Epochs]

    London Symphony and Ambrosian Singers,
Chávez conducting   Col. M. 32685

Obertura Republicana (Chapultepec)

    "Music of Mexico" The Symphony
Orchestra of Mexico, Chávez
conducting   Decca DL 9527

    The National Symphony Orchestra of
Mexico, Luis Herrera de la Fuente
conducting   Musart MCD 3017

Pirámide [Pyramid] Selections

    London Symphony and Ambrosian Singers,
Chávez conducting   Col. M 32685

Polígonos [Polygons]

    Hilde Somer, piano   Desto 6426

Preludes

    "Recital Mexicano," Miguel García (I, II, V,
       IX)   Musart MCD 3012

    "Musica Mexicana para Piano," Manuel
       Delaflor (I, II, V, VIII)   Angel SAM 35037

    Carlos Barajas (I, III, V)   Musart MCD 3028

    María Teresa Rodríguez (I, II, V, VII, X)   RCA ARL 1–3341

    "Latin-American Piano Music," Charlotte
       Martin (V)   Educo EP 3020

    "Música Americana Contemporanea," Jorgé
       Zulueta (I, V, VII)   Centro Argentino por la
                                             Libertad de la Cultura LP
                                             501

Sinfonía de Antígona

    "Carlos Chávez Conducts" The Stadium
       Orchestra of New York   Everest 3029

    "The Six Symphonies of Carlos Chávez"
       The National Symphony Orchestra of
       Mexico, Chávez conducting   Col. 3230064

Sinfonía Índia

    "Carlos Chávez Conducts" The Stadium
       Orchestra of New York   Everest 3029

    New York Philharmonic, Leonard Bernstein
       conducting   Col. MS–6514

    "Music of Mexico," The Symphony
       Orchestra of Mexico, Chávez
       conducting   Decca DL 9527

    "Carlos Chávez Directs Mexican Music,"
       Mexican Orchestra   CBS CLS–5369

    The National Symphony Orchestra of
       Mexico, Luis Herrera de la Fuente
       conducting   Musart MCD 3017

    The First Interamerican Festival Orchestra,
       Caracas, Chávez conducting   no number

"The Six Symphonies of Carlos Chávez,"
   The National Symphony Orchestra of
   Mexico, Chávez conducting   Col. 3230064

Soli I

   Thomas Stevens, trumpet, and members of
      the Westwood Wind Quintet   Crystal S S12

Solis I, II, and IV

   "Chávez Conducts Chávez," Chávez
      Ensemble   Odyssey Y–31534

Sonata No. 6

   Adrián Ruiz, piano   Genesis 1008

Sonatina for Violin and Piano

   Maro and Anahid Ajemian   MGM E 3180

Symphony No. 3

   "The Six Symphonies of Carlos Chávez,"
      The National Symphony Orchestra of
      Mexico, Chávez conducting   Col. 3230064

Symphony No. 4

   "Carlos Chávez Conducts" The Stadium
      Orchestra of New York   Everest 3029

   "The Six Symphonies of Carlos Chávez,"
      The National Symphony Orchestra of
      Mexico, Chávez conducting   Col. 3230064

Symphony No. 5 for strings

   MGM String Orchestra, Izler Solomon
      conducting   MGM E–3548

   "The Six Symphonies of Carlos Chávez,"
      The National Symphony Orchestra of
      Mexico, Chávez conducting   Col. 3230064

Symphony No. 6

   "The Six Symphonies of Carlos Chávez,"
      The National Symphony Orchestra of
      Mexico, Chávez conducting   Col. 3230064

Tambuco for six percussionists

  "Americana" Les Percussions de Strasbourg   Philips 6526 017

Three Pieces for Guitar

  "American Classics for Guitar," Turbio
    Sánchez   American Heritage Society AHS
    1445

  Manuel Barrueco   Turnabout 34678

Toccata for Percussion

  Los Angeles Percussion Ensemble, Henri
    Temianka conducting   Columbia 5847; CBS-Chile MS
    6447

  Boston Percussion Ensemble   Boston 207

  Concert Arts Orchestra, Felix Slatkin
    conducting   Capitol P-8299

  Gotham Percussionists   Urania 7144

  Manhattan Percussion Ensemble   Urania UX 134 (1034)

  MGM Chamber Orchestra, Izler Solomon
    conducting   MGM E 3155

  "Music for Percussion," vol. I, Tristan Fry
    Percussion Ensemble, John Eliot
    Gardiner conducting   Gale GMFD1–76–004

  "Americana" Les Percussions de Strasbourg   Philips 6526 017

Unidad [Unity]

  Hilde Somer, piano   Desto 6426

Xochipilli for four wind instruments and
  percussion

  "Carlos Chávez Directs Mexican Music,"
    Mexican Orchestra   CBS CLS–5369

Selected Bibliography

Primary Sources

Books and Parts of Books

Chávez, Carlos, "Mexican Music," in Hubert Herring and Herbert Weinstock, *Renascent Mexico*. New York: Covici-Friede, 1935, pp. 199–218.

———. "The Music of Mexico," in Henry Cowell, *American Composers on American Music*. New York: F. Ungar, 1962 (republication of Stanford University Press edition, 1933), pp. 102–106.

———. *Musical Thought*. Cambridge, Mass.: Harvard University Press, 1961. 126 pp. (Six Harvard lectures of 1958–1959).

———. *Toward a New Music*. New York: W.W. Norton & Co., 1937, 180 pp.

Articles

———. "Anatomic Analysis," *Piano Quarterly* 21, no. 3 (Summer, 1973):17–23

———. "The Function of the Concert," *Modern Music* 15, no. 2 (January-February, 1938):71–75.

———. "Iniciación a la Dirección de Orquesta," *Nuestra Música* 1, no. 4 (September, 1946):213–27; 2, no. 5 (January, 1947):5–18; 2, no. 6 (April, 1947):53–71; 3, no. 9 (January, 1948):5–10.

———. "Music for the Radio," *Modern Music* 17, no. 2 (January-February, 1941):87–92.

———. "Revolt in Mexico," *Modern Music* 13, no. 3 (March-April, 1936):35–40.

———. "La Sinfónica Nacional," *Nuestra Música* 5, no. 18 (2nd Trimester, 1950):111–37.

———. "The Two Persons," *Musical Quarterly* 15, no. 2 (April, 1929):153–59.

Published Lectures in Spanish

———. *El Arte Eleva*, Mexico City: Editorial de El Colegio Nacional, 1969. 18 pp.

———. *Debussy y la Guerra del 14*. Mexico City: Editorial de El Colegio Nacional, 1971. 14 pp.

———. *Etica y Estética*. Mexico City: Publicaciones de la Academia de Artes, 1971. 8 pp.

———. *Falla en México*. Mexico City: Editorial de El Colegio Nacional, 1970. 17 pp.

———. *Canto y Melodía; El Dodecafonismo en México. Sobretiro de la Memoria de El Colegio Nacional*. Mexico City: Editorial de El Colegio Nacional, 1954. pp. 65–71.

———. *Mis Amigos Poetas*. Mexico City: Editorial de El Colegio Nacional, 1977. 43 pp.

———. *Oro . . . No Vale; Lira de Orfeo*. Mexico City: Editorial de El Colegio Nacional, 1973. 19 pp.

Secondary Sources

Books and Parts of Books

Béhague, Gerard. *Music in Latin America: An Introduction.* Englewood Cliffs, N.J.: Prentice-Hall, 1979. 369 pp.

Béhague's book is the most complete survey of Latin American music to date. Musical discussions are well taken and liberally illustrated with choice examples, and each chapter is provided with suggested materials for further study.

Copland, Aaron. *The New Music.* New York: W.W. Norton, 1968. 194 pp. (revision of *Our New Music.* New York: McGraw-Hill, 1941).

Part I is a survey of contemporary American composers. In Part II, "Composers in America," Copland gives a thoughtful and authoritative assessment of Chávez's music.

Cowell, Henry. "Chávez," in *The Book of Modern Composers,* ed. David Ewen. New York: Alfred Knopf, 1950, pp. 443–46.

This is the same short article by Cowell found in the 1947 edition of Ewen's book, but the statement, "His blood is half Indian and half Spanish," is excised.

Ewen, David, ed. *The New Book of Modern Composers,* 3rd edition. New York: Alfred Knopf, 1961. 491 pp. (revision of the 1942 and 1950 editions entitled *The Book of Modern Composers*).

An excellent introduction by Nicolas Slonimsky is followed by chapters devoted to thirty-two individual composers. The chapter on Chávez has sections by Slonimsky, Chávez (from *Toward a New Music*), and Miriam Gideon.

———. *The World of Twentieth-Century Music.* Englewood Cliffs, N.J.: Prentice-Hall, 1968. 959 pp.

Many composers are included, but discussions are relatively brief: Chávez, pp. 156–160. *Resonancias* (1964) is the most recent work examined.

García Morillo, Roberto. *Carlos Chávez: Vida y Obra.* Mexico City and Buenos Aires: Fondo de Cultura Económica, 1960. 241 pp.

Argentine composer-critic García Morillo provides the most comprehensive and penetrating single book on Chávez and his musical life for the period before 1960. Its chronologically developed content benefits from direct contributions by the subject. The author includes an extensive list of writings by Chávez in the appendices.

Halffter, Rodolfo. *Carlos Chávez: Catalogo Completo de sus Obras.* Mexico City: Society of Authors and Composers of Music, 1971. 97 pp.

The most complete catalog of Chávez's music to date, this work includes music written as late as 1969, with information on instrumentations, commissions, and premiere performances. The chronological catalog is cross referenced with alphabetical and performance-media indexes.

Johnson, William Weber. *Heroic Mexico.* Garden City, N.Y.: Doubleday & Co., 1968. 463 pp.

This vivid and detailed account of the 1910 Revolution and Mexico's political history to the mid-1960s is helpful as a parallel resource in tracing Chávez's musical and administrative career.

Lichtenwanger, William and Carolyn, ed. *Modern Music, Published by the League of Composers, 1924–1946: An Analytical Index.* New York: AMS Press, 1976. 246 pp.

The Chávez student will find this catalog an indispensable key to the many references to the composer contained in editions of *Modern Music* since 1928.

Mayer-Serra, Otto. *The Present State of Music in Mexico.* Washington, D.C.: Organization of American States, 1960. 46 pp.

Mayer-Serra traces the development of musical nationalism from its folk roots to its transformation into universalism primarily at the hands of Chávez.

Mexican Music: Notes by Herbert Weinstock for Concerts Arranged by Carlos Chávez. New York: William E. Rudge's Sons, 1940. 31 pp.

Printed for the 1940 concerts of Mexican music presented with the Museum of Modern Art exhibit entitled "Twenty Centuries of Mexican Art," this program book sheds light on the folk music, nationalistic art music, indigenous instruments, etc., programmed in the concerts.

Music of Latin America. Washington, D.C.: Pan American Union, 1942. 57 pp. (Reprinted, 1975.)

This booklet surveys Latin American music from pre-Columbian times to 1942. Though Chávez is only briefly mentioned, his position is viewed comparatively with his Latin American contemporaries.

Newlon, Clarke. *The Men Who Made Mexico.* New York: Dodd-Mead & Co., 1973. 273 pp.

Chávez is the only musician included in this collection of biographical sketches of Mexican luminaries past and present. Some of the composer's contemporaries found in the book are Vasconcelos, Rivera, and cinema actor Cantinflas.

Orrego-Salas, Juan. ed. *Music from Latin America Available at Indiana University.* Bloomington: Indiana University Latin American Music Center, 1971. 412 pp.

Orrego-Salas, who directs the Latin American Music Center at Indiana University, has assembled this list of broad holdings. Chávez scores are listed on pages 35–37, and recordings (both commercial and noncommercial) on pages 222–27.

Rosenfeld, Paul. *By Way of Art.* New York: Coward-McCann, 1928. 309 pp.

Rosenfeld's chapter entitled "The Americanism of Carlos Chávez" (pp. 273–83) shows the attention the fledgling composer was receiving in New York in the mid-1920s.

Shanet, Howard. *Philharmonic: A History of New York's Orchestra.* New York: Doubleday & Co., 1975. 788 pp.

Shanet's exhaustive study of the New York Philharmonic provides pertinent details about Chávez's conducting engagements with the orchestra in 1937 and the commissioning of his *Symphony VI.*

Slonimsky, Nicolas. *Music of Latin America.* New York: Thomas Y. Crowell Co., 1945. 374 pp.

Part II of this book by Chávez's longtime friend and associate contains forty-one pages devoted to Mexican music, including an excellent section on indigenous instruments and a discussion of Chávez's music (pp. 230–35).

———. *Music Since 1900,* 4th edition. New York: W.W. Norton, 1971. 1595 pp.

Covering the period from 1900 to 1969, this compendium is a good source for premiere performances, festivals, and thumbnail descriptions of works.

Stevenson, Robert M. *Music in Aztec and Inca Territory.* Berkeley and Los Angeles: University of California Press, 1968. 378 pp.

Stevenson's thorough study of pre-Columbian music is an important stepping-stone in approaching Chávez's Mexican Indianism.

———. *Music in Mexico: A Historical Survey.* New York: Thomas Y. Crowell Co., 1952. 300 pp.

An excellent chronicle of early conducting and composing activity in Mexico, this study offers a look at Chávez's contributions to music in light of what preceded him.

21 Años de la Orquesta Sinfónica de México. Mexico City: 1948. 139 pp.

Francisco Agea compiled this statistical record of the twenty-one seasons of Chávez's orchestra. In its content are works performed, guest artists and conductors, premieres, orchestral personnel, and the maestro's yearly reports of progress and projections.

Articles

Modern Music (1924–1946), edited by Minna Lederman, is a rich source of periodical literature for Chávez and his music. Many of its articles were written by fellow composers who spoke with an authority gained by their grasp of the new musical currents around them. The frequent references to Chávez can be located through the excellent analytical catalog compiled by Wayne Shirley and edited by William and Carolyn Lichtenwanger (see under Books).

Bal y Gay, Jesús. "La Sinfonía de Antígona," *Nuestra Música* 5, no. 17 (1950):5–17.

Bal y Gay analyzes Chávez's "first" symphony and evaluates it as showing adequate proof of the composer's personal style.

―――. " 'La Hija de Cólquide' de Carlos Chávez," *Nuestra Música* 5, no. 19 (3rd Trimester, 1950):207–16.

The author limits his analysis, which is extensive, to the orchestral suite taken from the ballet music.

Sandi, Luis. "Cinquenta Años de Música en México," *Nuestra Música* 6, no. 23 (1951):248–59.

Mexican composer Sandi surveys the last fifty years of musical life in his country and concludes that Chávez is the most important musician of that period.

Devoto, Daniel. "Panorama de la Musicología Latinoamericano," *Acta Musicologica* 31, no. 3 (July-September, 1959):91–109.

Devoto's article is a useful bibliographic source for books and periodicals on music emanating from Latin America. Pages 94–97 cover music scholarship in Mexico.

Vega, Aurelio de la. "New World Composers," *Inter-American Music Bulletin* (Pan American Union publication also known as *Boletín Interamericano de Música*) 43 (September, 1964):1–6.

This compact article gives a quick overview of composers in the Americas since the Spanish Conquest. A point is made (p. 6) that in Mexico the gap left by Chávez and Revueltas and after Galindo's generation is yet to be filled.

Weinstock, Herbert. "Carlos Chávez," *Composers of the Americas* (Pan American Union) 3 (1960):60–83.

Weinstock's article first appeared in *Musical Quarterly* 22, no. 4 (October, 1936), and was modified by him in 1944 and 1956. The succinct biographical section is followed by a clear discussion of stylistic development and a classified catalog of works.

Music Dictionaries

"Carlos Chávez," *Baker's Biographical Dictionary of Musicians,* 6th edition, revised by Nicolas Slonimsky. New York: Schirmer Books, 1978. pp. 308–9.

Slonimsky lists premiere performance dates of works in addition to a capsulized biographical account. Some of the late works are not included.

Carmona, Gloria. "Carlos Chávez." *Dictionary of Contemporary Music.* New York: E. P. Dutton, 1974, pp. 135–37.

Mexican writer Gloria Carmona distils the essence of Chávez's stylistic development into an article replete with accurate factual information presented from an informed position.

Chase, Gilbert. "Carlos Chávez." *The New Grove Dictionary of Music and Musicians,* 6th edition, Stanley Sadie, ed. New York: Macmillan, 1980. Vol. IV, pp. 185–88.

Renowned Latin American music scholar Gilbert Chase presents up-to-date biography, list of writings, bibliography, and list of works and traces the evolution of style in Chávez's music.

Dissertations and Theses

Coombs, Joan Sweeney. "Carlos Chávez: A Reassessment of his Place in Twentieth-Century Music." Master's thesis, University of Alabama, 1981.

Ms. Coombs attempts to show the degree of alignment between Chávez's stated musical values and the music written concurrently. Special emphasis is placed on the more experimental works after 1950.

Igou, Orin Lincoln. "Contemporary Symphonic Activity in Mexico with Special Regard to Carlos Chávez and Silvestre Revueltas." Ph.D. dissertation, Northwestern University, 1946 (Library of Congress film: 783.109). 593 pp.

Written too early to offer much in the way of Chávez scholarship, the study has value for stylistic comparison of the composer with his popular contemporary Revueltas.

Malmström, Dan. *Introduction to Twentieth-Century Mexican Music.* Ph.D. dissertation, Uppsala University, 1974 (distributed through the Institute of Musicology, Uppsala University, Uppsala, Sweden). 167 pp.

Discussion of music in the Revolutionary epoch (1910–1920) follows a brief historical background. The music of Chávez and some of his pupils is treated extensively. There is also a limited discography and list of works.

Parker, Robert L. "The Development of the Symphonic Style of Carlos Chávez as Evidenced by Three of his Symphonies." Master's thesis, The University of Texas, 1956. 103 pp.

The composer's first three symphonies are subjected to analysis of form, melody, harmony, rhythm, and instrumentation. The thesis concludes with a synthesis of style elements shared by these three works.

Index